HACKING
CULTURALLY
INCLUSIVE
TEACHING

8 Anti-Racist Strategies to Help Teachers and Leaders Improve Equity in Education

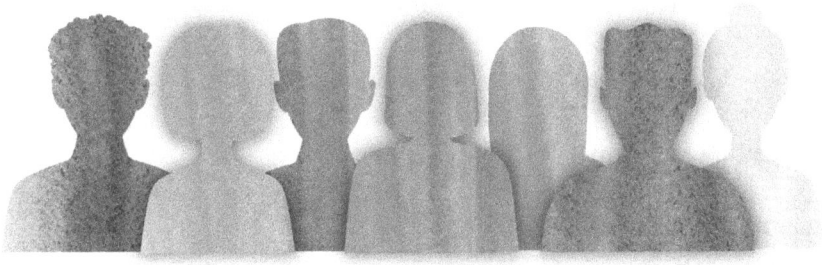

HACK™ Learning SERIES

KENDRA
NALUBEGA-BOOKER

Hacking Culturally Inclusive Teaching
© 2023 by Times 10 Publications
Highland Heights, OH 44143 USA
Website: 10publications.com

Cover and Interior Design by Steven Plummer
Editing by Jen Z. Marshall
Copyediting by Jennifer Jas

Paperback ISBN: 978-1-956512-30-4
eBook ISBN: 978-1-956512-31-1
Hardcover ISBN: 978-1-956512-32-8

Library of Congress Cataloging-in-Publication Data is available for this title.

First Printing: April 2023

I dedicate this book to those before me, the ones during my time, and those after me who continue fighting for social justice to create a better world for our children.

CONTENTS

CREATING A CULTURALLY INCLUSIVE CLASSROOM

To truly begin to understand, appreciate, and address the impact of racism in K–12 education, we must begin to assess our schools, classrooms, and programs through an anti-racist lens.
— Dr. Adrienne D. Dixson

BEFORE MOVING TO the United States in 2010, I studied in Uganda for fourteen years as a first-generation African student and learned to speak four languages: English, Luganda, Kinyarwanda, and Swahili. Upon arrival in the US, I took the WIDA exam to measure my English language proficiency and placed in Level 3 (Developing) of the English for Speakers of Other Languages (ESL) program. I attended an Illinois community college before transferring to a four-year public university.

These distinct educational institutions exposed me to various pedagogical approaches. Considering how they impacted my academic success and linguistic skills as a multilingual student, some practices in these institutions benefited me, while others were detrimental to my education.

I have spoken English since the first grade because it is the language of instruction in Uganda. While attending English Language Learner classes in the United States, I felt isolated because none of the instructors spoke my native languages. This is typical for minority languages, particularly African languages, in the US. For this reason, I always completed assignments on my own, and I did exceptionally well! The assignment did not correspond with my linguistic abilities, and the classes held a wide range of proficiency. Some teachers asked me, "What is a Black girl doing in ESL?" and I did not know how to respond.

My counselor attempted to determine why, since my English was "good."

The placement perplexed my parents. I wished to be in a class that would engage and motivate me to learn. My mother insisted on enrolling me in mainstream classes, but she had no idea how the system worked. During my junior year of high school, I finally tested out of ESL and joined "mainstream" classes, and I felt that I was finally adequately challenged. The material matched my level of expertise. In fact, I earned all As in my last semester of classes and graduated early. I exerted more effort than before to demonstrate my fluent English and show that I belonged in classrooms that corresponded to my proficiency level. That burden of proof falls outside the scope of student responsibility, yet I carried it.

My identity as a Black immigrant made the experience more complicated, especially considering my high school's predominantly White neighborhood. I've always wondered if my experience would have been different if I had attended a diverse school. Now that I have had the opportunity to teach and mentor culturally and linguistically diverse students (CLDs), I can say that the development of my linguistic insecurities partially resulted from my ELL program's deficit-approach strategies. You can learn more about moving away from this mentality in the book *Hacking Deficit Thinking*.

I felt that my English would never be adequate, which caused me to overcorrect myself. Some of my peers who were also classified as ELLs at one point shared my sentiments. They felt that certain teaching methods hindered their educational experience rather than enhanced it. I began to realize that there are students like me who have yet to find an educator who understands them and can assist them in achieving academic success without making them feel unimportant.

These experiences fueled my desire to become an educator and work with diverse students. I want to be the change that my fourteen-year-old self needed and all CLDs require today. My goal is to enhance student learning experiences both inside and outside of the classroom by creating communities of practicum and fostering an environment where students are comfortable making mistakes and where they feel valued and understood. I want all students, regardless of their cultural and linguistic backgrounds, to feel like they belong and can succeed.

I am committed to researching and identifying means to accommodate diverse students and level the playing field for their academic and professional success. I am committed to working in this area. Educators and leaders can develop and implement strategies that engage students in the learning process, amplify their voices, and motivate them to use higher-level critical thinking skills while also promoting meaningful, equitable learning experiences. It is my responsibility, as an educator, to reflect on my experiences and understand newer generations of CLDs and to promote effective anti-racist pedagogical practices that other educators can consider as they transform their classrooms.

I've worked in education for over nine years in high schools, community colleges, and four-year universities. I spent more than two years teaching college-level and high school students and over four years developing courses for diverse populations on a systemwide scale. I have spearheaded education solutions at a top technology company. Renowned education scholars and researchers such as Dr. Arlette Willis, Dr. Adrienne Dixson, Dr. Ann Haas Dyson, and others trained me during my doctoral program, where I studied learning and literacy issues and conducted research. In addition to briefly training pre-service teachers, I have collaborated with other educators, parents, researchers, community organizers, after-school programs, and nonprofit organizations.

Given my personal journey and our current educational climate, writing this book is an organic next step in my career and life. It is an honor and a great responsibility for me to finally share my experience and the solutions I've always desired to see in the classroom and in education overall.

Culturally and linguistically diverse students are underrepresented and excluded in the classroom, according to research rooted in anti-racist frameworks, such as culturally relevant teaching, culturally sustaining pedagogies, and raciolinguistics. We underrepresent, stigmatize, undervalue, and erase cultures and languages in our educational system, directly impacting academic trajectories and how students situate themselves in the world outside the classroom. In *Hacking Culturally Inclusive Teaching*, I offer research-based recommendations and best practices from diverse in-service teachers to assist educators in improving teaching and outcomes for culturally and linguistically diverse students and racialized students.

INTENDED AUDIENCE

This book is a resource for developing culturally relevant, inclusive, and sustainable curricula and instruction to improve outcomes for CLDs and racialized students. It allows students and teachers to collaborate on knowledge creation while promoting accessible and equitable learning. Transform your teaching by using these student-centered, anti-racist pedagogical methods. Although the book focuses on multilingual students, you can use the strategies with all students. According to the National Center for Education Statistics, the United States population has become more diverse over the last two decades, requiring teachers to better prepare for working with CLDs in their classrooms.

HOW TO USE THIS BOOK

When it comes to teaching CLDs, a one-size-fits-all approach does not exist, but we can include every student in the learning process and meet their unique needs. Each chapter offers a step-by-step approach to incorporating culturally inclusive practices. You can use tangible, impactful strategies for your students in addition to overcoming pushbacks. Consider how you could modify each problem and hack for the benefit of your students and to improve your teaching techniques as you read through each one. It can be difficult to break old habits. However, by continuing to prioritize our students' needs, we can challenge ineffective methods and make room for improvement. All you need is an open mind and the willingness to try new ideas. This book can help educators begin or improve their current instruction.

HOW THIS BOOK IS UNIQUE

There is a growing body of literature on incorporating culturally inclusive and sustaining teaching practices. However, a gap exists in their actual implementation. Traditional methods continue to heavily emphasize White-dominant culture and assimilating students. We need more support and resources for racialized students, who face unique challenges in the classroom due to the underrepresentation of their cultural and linguistic backgrounds. This book is different because it was written by a former English as a Second

Language (ESL) student and current educator who is a multilingual African immigrant. It draws on research and experience to address contemporary issues in practice pertaining to leveraging students' prior knowledge and developing culturally sustainable environments. Building on anti-racist literature, *Hacking Culturally Inclusive Teaching* proposes ideas for changing problematic or ineffective styles rather than changing students' cultures and linguistics. It relieves racialized students of the pressure to assimilate or modify themselves to "fit" the dominant culture. It provides teachers with steps to create more welcoming, inclusive classrooms. This book is a resource for educators who wish to empower and support diverse students, challenge problematic practices, and foster critical thinking.

A note on terminology: I interchangeably refer to racialized students and culturally and linguistically diverse students (CLDs). Both terms refer to essentially the same student population, though not all racialized students are multilingual.

Recent political debates have surrounded the teaching of social justice-related topics, such as Critical Race Theory (CRT), in law school. The topic has become "taboo" in schools, making it a challenge for teachers at all levels to pursue equity training. Because so much misinformation is out there, it is important to clarify the topic for those who are unfamiliar with CRT. It is a legal academic framework that looks at the interplay between race, power, and law and examines how racism manifests in culture and society, as well as how it affects different groups of people. It also focuses on how minoritized groups can work together to challenge power structures and create long-term social change.

Some parents and guardians have expressed concerns about their children's exposure to CRT, believing that K–12 schools teach students the theory, although it remains a law school subject. Related legislation in many states has led to tensions.

Teachers generally want to provide a safe, inclusive space for all students. They feel torn between policy, practice inconsistencies, and cultural miscommunications. They expect pushback from different directions: leadership, parents, students, and their colleagues. Regardless of the current political climate, teachers must continue to push efforts to eliminate equity gaps, adopt an equality mindset, and foster safe environments that address issues in a developmentally appropriate way.

As a teacher, you can reflect on why these debates even exist in the first place. How are current responses from government and education leaders shaping the learning experience for your diverse students? Social justice issues affect all aspects of our students' lives. We cannot ignore what is happening if we truly want to create a just learning environment for them. If teachers aren't well-prepared, a cultural gap opens up between them and their students, making it harder for educators to choose effective teaching methods and curriculum materials.

HACK 1

SHIFT TOWARD BRAVE SPACES
Design an Authentic Environment

The goal of a safe classroom space is to create a climate where students are willing to "risk honesty" so that an authentic exchange of ideas becomes possible. Brave spaces are used today in classroom settings as a mechanism to create supportive environments so that all students may equally participate in challenging dialogue.
– National Association of Student Personnel Administrators

THE PROBLEM: CLASSROOMS ARE NOT ALWAYS SAFE SPACES FOR RACIALIZED STUDENTS

OFTEN, WHEN RACIALIZED students express strong emotions and views or share harsh glimpses of their everyday experiences, members of the dominant group may feel unsafe, become uncomfortable, or react defensively. This further pushes students and teachers into comfort zones that get in the way of real learning or confronting issues that go beyond classroom boundaries. Even if your school doesn't allow you to directly address the issues, the way you treat students will impact how they perceive each other outside of the classroom.

The difference between a safe space and a brave space is that a safe space is historically created and guarded by racialized communities—and they protect it by dictating who can and cannot be in these spaces. On the other hand, brave spaces can be any space that challenges anyone to participate honestly in sensitive topics, even with the risk of becoming problematic or offensive. The phrase "safe space" became loosely used and sometimes confused with "brave space." In a safe classroom, students and teachers can participate in thought-provoking conversations without being held accountable when they offend others or perpetuate racism or other-isms because it is "safe"—unlike brave spaces, which allow for accountability and responsibility for what we say and do.

Although it is easier to maintain the traditional curriculum, we miss out on truly supporting our students, whose histories and current realities misalign with the "traditional" curriculum. True transformation comes from pushing limits and challenging ourselves and our students to grow. We need more "brave" classroom spaces, making it a top priority for us to create these spaces and set a firm foundation for inclusive teaching.

THE HACK: SHIFT TOWARD BRAVE SPACES

First used by Brian Arao and Kristi Clemens in their book *The Art of Effective Facilitation: Reflections from Social Justice Educators*, the term "brave spaces" has since gained widespread usage. They suggested five key components to creating a brave space in education.

- **Controversy with civility** encourages students to express their opinions while respecting others' perspectives, despite their differences.

- When **owning intentions and impacts**, students consider how their words have affected the emotions of others.

- Students engage in conversations that may be challenging for them when they opt to be **challenged by choice**.

- Students practice **respect** or mutual regard for one another's dignity as human beings.

- Students agree to not maliciously inflict harm on one another when they commit to the **no attacks** component.

When teachers and students allow themselves to be vulnerable in class, they actively choose to foster more meaningful connections between themselves and their peers. To meet the challenges as educators, we can work to unlearn problematic perspectives and ideas that lead to unjust actions.

It is vital for students to belong to a community that is trusting, empathetic, and connected.

You can transform your classroom into a brave space. Position it by setting classroom rules or codes: what you allow and what you don't. Promote critical thinking, growth, and empathy.

As educators, we can recognize that all students bring unique experiences and backgrounds to the classroom and that they can all learn from each other. In the same sense, we realize that not all experiences are equal, especially when it comes to the lived experiences of racialized students. Let's aim for holistic education: asking about students' languages and cultures, engaging them, sparking conversations about current events, promoting diverse ways of learning, and challenging students to think critically on a local, national, and global level. While not all schools and districts allow teachers to delve into the more controversial issues, most teachers can subtly get the point across by allowing students to share their experiences with each other.

WHAT YOU CAN DO TOMORROW

- **Reflect on the answers to big-picture questions.**
  What would a brave space mean for my students? How should I prepare? How will such a space impact my teaching? What challenges should I expect? Do I have any ground rules for navigating difficult conversations? How do I handle sensitive topics in my classroom? Do my students feel comfortable participating? What needs to change? Who speaks up, and who is silent or silenced?

- **Set an example with an initial brave space activity.**
  Successfully turning your classroom into a brave space requires a long-term commitment, but you can begin tomorrow with this activity. Ask your students to sit in community-style circle seating, and start a conversation about what it means to be brave. You and your students can come up with a class definition based on responses. Ask students

to think back to a time when they felt brave. Then, ask them to talk about the thoughts, images, feelings, or actions that came to mind. You could also ask them to create a project or image that shows a time when they were brave, even if it meant they might offend others. You may want to allow them to use their mobile devices, such as an iPad and an Apple Pencil, to create their images.

Ask students to explore the following questions:

> ▸ Have you ever done something brave at school? What was it, and why did you do it?
>
> ▸ For this classroom, what do you need to be brave?
>
> ▸ Go around answering the questions as a class and ask students to document responses in a shared Google document that everyone can access.
>
> ▸ Finally, ask the students to make a list of rules for being brave in the classroom based on what they have talked about and shared.

- **Explore goals for an open-minded environment.** It's essential to meet students where they are instead of setting unrealistic expectations. If you are new to transforming your classrooms in this way, use the SMART goal format to guide you (see Appendix A.1). That structure offers an extra piece of strategic planning that allows you to have tangible success measures as you implement this new approach. It is not always a necessary step for everyone, but it makes it easy for students to also set personal development goals. Ask yourself the following questions as you and your students set your goals:

- ‣ Does the objective identify a specific improvement area?
- ‣ Does it specify how to measure and evaluate success?
- ‣ Is it relevant to the creation and maintenance of a brave space?
- ‣ Is it constrained by a predetermined timeline?

- **Give and require mutual respect.** The classroom is a community that requires mutual respect, deep and critical thinking about human experiences, and a toolkit for students to use beyond the classroom. Students and teachers can use this toolkit to be allies to their racialized counterparts, and racialized students can exist without taking on a burden. By creating a brave space, we invite all conversations, difficult or not, and emphasize learning through honest reflections. This practice can be hard to navigate, but it is necessary because it allows students to connect societal experiences with learning and to develop skills beyond the classroom. It also amplifies the human experience that sometimes gets clouded when we shield students from the "real world" and avoid conversations about social injustices, educational inequities, and other forms of oppression that affect racialized students and teachers. While your school or district may not allow you to address any of these items directly, you can set up your students for success by discussing them outside of the school environment.

Implement these idea starters with your students:

- ▸ Listen to and value their thoughts and ideas.
- ▸ Acknowledge and respond to their feelings.
- ▸ Treat all students equally and fairly.
- ▸ Use appropriate language and avoid sarcasm.
- ▸ Give students choices in learning activities and assignments.
- ▸ Encourage and praise their efforts and accomplishments.
- ▸ Respect their opinions and beliefs.
- ▸ Avoid making assumptions about their backgrounds.
- ▸ Involve students in problem-solving and decision-making.
- ▸ Respect their privacy and confidentiality.

- **Curate a list of questions to guide you as you create your first brave space classroom.** Brave spaces allow maximizing learning through others' experiences and recognizing counter-stories usually shared in safe spaces. Racialized students and teachers do not always feel comfortable sharing their stories, so put predetermined conditions in place for them to be vulnerable. We all can benefit from developing brave spaces; the next section provides ideas on how to integrate them into culturally inclusive and sustaining learning environments. Consider these examples:

▸ What are my expectations for student behavior?

▸ How can I create an environment that supports diverse backgrounds and opinions?

▸ What strategies can I use to foster a sense of trust and respect among my students?

▸ How can I encourage my students to feel comfortable speaking up and engaging in meaningful dialogue?

▸ How do I ensure accountability when students offend others?

▸ How can I promote collaboration and creativity in the brave space classroom?

▸ How can I make the brave space classroom an inclusive and safe space for all students?

▸ How can I create an atmosphere of acceptance and understanding?

▸ How can I address any issues of bias and discrimination that may arise?

▸ How do I use technology and other resources to enhance my brave space classroom?

- **Set up the classroom in a community-style circle.** Experiment with placements that bring everyone together. The community-style classroom format focuses on students working together to explore, discuss, and solve problems. This type of classroom approach encourages students to collaborate and learn from each other to reach a common goal. It also emphasizes communication, critical thinking, and problem-solving skills. In this format, students sit in a circle or around a table, allowing everyone an equal opportunity to participate. The teacher acts as a facilitator, helping students understand the concepts and come up with solutions. This type of classroom setting gives students the opportunity to learn from their peers and build relationships and trust. It is vital for students to belong to a community that is trusting, empathetic, and connected. Students should have the freedom to stand, lean, bounce, and move as they see fit.

Adjust furniture to create an inviting space that gives students more opportunities to interact with each other and actively participate in the learning environment, especially since racialized students may feel uncomfortable engaging in White-dominated, traditional classroom settings. Students benefit from having a choice since it gives them the freedom to work wherever and however they see fit. When they feel isolated, they are less likely to participate.

Make the environment more inviting by arranging desks in a semi-circle or full circle, with the teacher sitting among students. Include comfortable chairs and a desk arrangement that encourages conversation, with some desks facing each other. You can display student-created colorful art and inspiring posters on the walls. Scatter plants and small sculptures around the room. Help students to feel comfortable engaging in meaningful conversations in a relaxed and inviting atmosphere.

- **Explain why it's essential to establish brave spaces.** Once students understand what you are trying to create, they may start thinking about how and what they can contribute to this space. Their curiosity will spark, and they may have questions about what this means for them. Assure them this approach will enrich everyone's learning.

  Choose a method of accountability. Abide by the rules or codes and ensure that everyone, including you, has access to the agreed-upon rules. You can choose to record your rules on a smart board or shared document where you can allow everyone to brainstorm ideas.

- **Model characteristics of a brave space.** When you are vulnerable or show empathy toward your students, they're more likely to follow your lead. This doesn't mean everyone must share opinions that they do not feel comfortable sharing. Instead, it invites students to share their ideas, feelings, and thoughts. They must challenge themselves to share as a way to enrich their learning. It also promotes honesty, trust, and a sense of community. More specifically, if someone says or does something deemed offensive, racist, or discriminatory, it should not be sugar-coated or brushed over to play it safe. Instead, address it and see it as an opportunity.

RESPECT EVERYONE REGARDLESS OF RACE, SEX, GENDER, LANGUAGE, SOCIO-ECONOMIC STATUS, ETC.

ACTIVELY LISTEN TO EACH OTHER WITHOUT INTERRUPTION.

ASK QUESTIONS INSTEAD OF ASSUMING.

SPEAK YOUR MIND AND SHARE YOUR OPINIONS AND PERSPECTIVES, BUT BE OPEN AND **PREPARED TO BE CHALLENGED.**

ALL DEROGATORY TERMS ARE FORBIDDEN IN THIS CLASSROOM, AND ANYONE WHO USES THEM WILL FACE DISCIPLINARY ACTION.

Image 1.1: Expectations in a brave space classroom.

A BLUEPRINT FOR FULL IMPLEMENTATION

STEP 1: Adopt and maintain a brave space mindset.

Prepare to challenge thoughts that arise when creating an inclusive space that welcomes diverse ideas and opinions in your classroom. Actively model brave behavior. Embrace mistakes as learning opportunities; a brave space teacher is willing to make mistakes and use them as an opportunity for growth.

Aim to create an environment where students feel comfortable taking risks without worrying about judgment or criticism from their peers or the teacher. Actively seek and value diverse perspectives. By facilitating open dialogue, you encourage conversation between students and create a space where they feel comfortable expressing their thoughts and ideas without fear of judgment. Brave space teachers promote self-reflection and strive to help students gain insight into their thoughts and feelings. Respect and value the diversity of your students and ensure everyone feels included and appreciated in the classroom.

STEP 2: Measure student development as you create your inclusive space.

Once you set your goals, you can use them as the basis to measure your and your students' development over time as you build your culturally inclusive space. As educators, we spend a lot of time planning, but we also know that learning does not always go as planned because it requires being flexible for the sake of our learners, and, of course, it takes time. By streamlining planning and execution processes, we can more efficiently adjust our plan depending on student progress and understanding. Be flexible and allow yourself time to try new methods. You want to spend less time planning and more time building a community and creating flexible learning.

STEP 3: Teach through the lens of intersectionality.

According to Kimberlé Crenshaw, a civil rights advocate, intersectionality refers to the connections, overlaps, and influences that identity-based systems of privilege and oppression have on one another on social, economic, and political levels. Intersectionality, in its broadest sense, describes how the mingling of various social identities has a distinctive impact on people's lived experiences. When you teach students about intersectionality, you provide a theoretical framework for them to comprehend how personal lived experiences and those of other people relate to a larger social structure of privilege and oppression.

Intersectionality is an essential tool in creating a brave space learning environment because it provides a way to examine and understand individuals' identities and experiences. It allows for a more inclusive and practical learning experience through a deeper understanding of how different identities and experiences intersect and interact with each other. By using an intersectionality lens, educators are better equipped to recognize and address the unique needs of each student. This approach fosters an environment of empathy, understanding, and respect. Additionally, intersectionality helps create a learning space that is more diverse and inclusive so all students can feel safe, seen, and heard.

Give students structures to use as they explore the ways in which their identities and oppressions overlap with the course content. Create exercises that encourage students to consider how factors such as race, age, culture, family dynamics, homophobia, and racism all intersect. Involve students and guide them to what they find meaningful in the curriculum so they can discuss topics that interest them. If you're in a more restricted environment, find ways to subtly suggest challenges people have that your students may not have considered. To learn strategies for teaching kids about empathy, politics, and civic responsibility, see the book *Preventing Polarization* by Michelle Blanchet and Brian Deters.

STEP 4: Prioritize students' mental well-being.

Promoting well-being in the classroom is closely related to social justice because it helps create an equitable learning environment where all students feel respected and valued, no matter their background or identity. By providing resources and tools that support mental health and well-being, teachers help all students gain access to the support they need to be successful. In addition, prioritizing well-being in the classroom can help reduce the stigma associated with mental health and create an environment of acceptance and understanding that considers the lived experience of all students, especially racialized students.

You can model positive self-talk through affirmations to support students' mental health and influence their personal growth and development. Demonstrate the significance of positive affirmations and provide personal examples of how this leads to effective results. Students will begin to understand that they can train and strengthen their minds through intentional work on themselves. This can boost their intellect, help them cope with other hardships they may be facing, and strengthen them on a mental and spiritual level. You can find an example lesson plan in Appendix A.2.

STEP 5: Incorporate mindfulness activities in the classroom routine.

Mindfulness activities can include deep breathing, guided meditation, or yoga. Hold regular check-ins with students to get a sense of how they are feeling. Create activities that foster positive relationships between students, and practice positive reinforcement techniques to recognize and reward good behavior and effort. Model and encourage a discussion about emotions in a safe and supportive environment. Talk about mindfulness and self-care practices that will build healthy coping strategies they can call upon when needed. Encourage physical activities and discuss mental health and well-being with an open and honest dialogue.

STEP 6: Address offensive comments.

You will have moments when students will say offensive words to or about each other. For starters, you must communicate the need for respect, among other rules, at the beginning of the school year so students know there will be consequences for inappropriate actions—it's a massive part of an open, transparent brave space. Like you, your students will always have their own prejudices, presumptions, and biases, so you must be ready to stop potentially offensive statements so other students feel free to be themselves in class.

Stop and address the issue immediately. If any time passes, it seems less important. Explain why the comments or actions are harmful and go against equity, inclusion, and diversity or promote a form of -ism. Openly discuss the issue privately with the student.

At this point, emphasize a zero-tolerance policy for behavior that doesn't promote an equitable classroom. Follow up with parents or guardians and the school's leadership as needed.

Check in with the student or students who felt offended by the comment or action. The last part is a huge priority. We often become so lost in communicating only with the student who committed the offense that we forget the most essential part, which is advocating for vulnerable students and nurturing their holistic well-being. How you react matters to the students and can strongly impact their lives beyond that moment.

STEP 7: Revise and improve the following school year.

Keep a record of what worked and what did not. Allow students to provide feedback. Compare your feedback with that of your students. Make a plan and revise it with future students to ensure that it aligns with that particular class and the community you are building together or make necessary changes together.

OVERCOMING PUSHBACK

In a brave space, the focus is on creating a safe and supportive learning environment for everyone, where mistakes can be made without fear of judgment and all are encouraged to speak openly and honestly. One would think that everyone could agree on the value of that classroom environment; however, some people are stuck on continuing a traditional learning environment where the focus is on assessment and student performance with less emphasis on creating a safe, supportive learning atmosphere. You may hear pushback from those who resist change, even good change. Here are comments you might hear and responses you might share.

I don't want my child to discuss race or sensitive topics. Complex topics will happen in and out of the classroom, and they will be especially challenging for students unequipped with the tools to engage with issues that are a part of other students' daily lives. The classroom is an ideal space because students have a chance to develop and grow in ways that future workplaces or other spaces may not afford. Give parents a heads-up about the topics you will cover by sharing the curriculum or simply communicating with them, as you already do. Make sure they understand that each student's background and entire existence (identity, language, culture) adds a lot of value to the classroom and that you are creating a space where students' diverse identities can coexist. For students to learn from each other's lived experiences, they can practice being open-minded, and it's a quality that can also be practiced at home. Reassure the parents that, as a teacher, you are helping their child have healthy conversations that are right for their age and are important for the classroom and the real world.

Assure parents that you'll be opening up a forum for the students, not using this system as a means to convey your ideology.

Unengaged students do not want to share their experiences, cultures, or languages in the classroom. Avoid putting students on the spot or making racialized students in the classroom feel like "native informants and unpaid sherpas," assigning racialized groups the responsibility to guide White students to a racial awakening. It's best to be patient with students and respect their comfort levels. Try engaging them in small-group activities or giving them alternatives that make them feel more comfortable expressing themselves and eventually participating. Students are more likely to share and talk among their peers than share aloud with the entire class, especially at the beginning of the school year when they are still getting to know you and their peers. It takes time to warm up and be vulnerable, but it is also okay if the student does not share personal information, as long as they do all the other assigned activities.

Students only share cookie-cutter answers, and none of them want to dig deeper. Start setting high expectations at the beginning of the school year. Prepare students for follow-up questions when they share short responses that sound like they are directly regurgitated from a reading or from someone else. You can follow up with questions like: How did you come to that conclusion? Can you explain your thought process to me? How does that relate to the different materials we have covered in the classroom? Can you explain it from a counter-perspective? These types of questions keep students prepared and help them think more critically.

I don't think this practice will serve all my students. Brave spaces encourage all teachers and students to unlearn negative viewpoints or concepts that motivate unjust behavior. All students can help establish classroom norms or regulations, defining what is acceptable and what is not, and encouraging critical thinking, personal development, and empathy. Everyone's voice is heard and encouraged.

THE HACK IN ACTION

Ms. Char'Li Ali, an African American teacher in Chicago, impacts students by embedding prompted journaling as an intimate brave space in her classroom practices. When we spoke, it was her second year teaching her class, but she has been in education for four years. Her class is composed of all Black students from the South Side of Chicago.

Ali's goals for an inclusive, equitable classroom were for students to look forward to coming to class—or at least not dread it every day. She does not want her classroom to be a place where they hate to be. She continues to create a fair place where everyone can share their voice and every student knows that they matter. Her classroom is an excellent example of anti-racist, culturally inclusive, relevant, and sustainable pedagogy. Even her students have *mentioned* to her how much they enjoy coming to school. Some have added that journaling takes the longest part of their day, but they enjoy it. Journaling has created a valuable classroom culture.

She gives them a journal question or prompt, typically about themselves or their lives, and allocates time for them to write. After students complete their writing, they go around the classroom and share their answers. Although it takes a long time, Ali understands the importance of this activity because each person's voice is heard. She describes it as getting a piece of everybody's life that you normally would not because students probably do not ask each other those kinds of questions outside of the classroom (or even outside of their small circle of friends). It is a great way for them to get to know each other on a deeper level and for her to get to know the students. Ali and her students have learned from journal share-aloud because students are becoming increasingly eager to share their journals. They are closer, which fosters an environment where everyone feels included and their voices and experiences are valued.

Ali's class demographic is not as common in many schools across the US unless the school is in a predominantly Black neighborhood. Your class may look totally different, yielding different results in student engagement and how comfortably they share their stories, but that only reinforces the importance of journaling in the classroom. This brave space allows students to show up authentically, feel respected, experience vulnerability, and embrace a classroom culture of sharing personal stories. Although one may argue that it is a safe space due to her class being all Black students, each student has unique experiences that make Ali's classroom even more diverse.

As educators, we are aware that each student has different experiences and backgrounds, and we can use these differences to let students be themselves and share their viewpoints and experiences in the brave spaces of our classrooms. All will benefit in school and in life when we understand more about each other. In a similar vein, we acknowledge that not all experiences are created equal, particularly when it comes to the real-world encounters of students who identify as racialized. You will most likely have moments when you need to remind students (and yourself) about this space you are creating. Refer to the shared rules and codes when necessary. Continue to reinforce your brave space beyond the introduction; the more it becomes a part of the classroom community, the more students will gain from it, and it will become a foundation for challenging an oppressive society beyond their classroom walls.

CO-CREATE KNOWLEDGE

Collaborate to Foster Student-Centered Learning

*Teachers and students (leadership and people),
co-intent on reality, are both subjects, not only in
the task of unveiling that reality, and thereby coming
to know it critically, but in the task of re-creating
that knowledge. As they attain this knowledge of
reality through common reflection and action, they
discover themselves as its permanent re-creators.*
— PAULO FREIRE, AUTHOR OF *PEDAGOGY OF THE OPPRESSED*

THE PROBLEM: OUR STRUCTURE LEAVES LITTLE ROOM FOR COLLABORATION

SOME TEACHERS HAVE little to no collaboration with their students when planning classroom activities and materials. Relying on traditional practices that favor the predominant culture hinders efforts to develop culturally responsive and inclusive environments because of its exclusive nature. In classrooms that incorporate co-creation to some extent, however, students may find it difficult to transition between the roles of learner and co-creator due to the differences between them. Since students are rarely exposed to the full co-creation process, it may be difficult for them to comprehend their roles, and this can cause them to feel unsure. Traditional pedagogical practices limit students' ability to conceptualize new instructional strategies in a co-creating classroom. We may need to help students hone their interpersonal and communication skills to participate in well-balanced, sustainable collaborative environments with teachers.

Paulo Freire, a Brazilian educator and one of the most prominent educational philosophers of the late twentieth century, argued for education systems emphasizing learning as a cultural and liberating act. He is best known for concepts like the banking model, where passive students receive pre-curated knowledge. He speaks to conscientization, which refers to the learner's progress toward an awareness of the power dynamics that shape our lives, the ability to think critically about the causes of social injustice and inequality, and the courage to take action to create positive change. He emphasizes the culture of silence in which minoritized students lose the ability to critically challenge the dominant culture.

> *Co-creating knowledge with students provides an excellent foundation for all students because it permits cultural infusion in the process.*

These concepts emerged as a response to the problematic structures of schooling that we continue to see in education today. When the learning community excludes students, it further supports the banking model, disrupting students' abilities to become critical thinkers and problem-solvers. They do not see themselves as part of the solution, which causes them to engage less and less—eventually becoming silent.

Co-creation encourages students to innovate and create solutions, which opens up numerous exciting opportunities to transform education. However, as students learn new concepts and skills (in which they are not subject matter or pedagogy experts), they feel unsure about their knowledge and abilities or unprepared to advance to higher levels of learning. Then, they are less likely to engage with learning materials and more likely to develop anxiety and avoid taking risks. To combat this, teachers must train students to take risks, nurture their ideas, and support them by setting the standard and modeling what inclusive, collaborative learning looks like. Implementing co-creation might induce apprehension in teachers because it requires them to reconsider their understanding of the roles of students and teachers.

THE HACK: CO-CREATE KNOWLEDGE

Co-creation means teachers and students share the responsibilities of teaching and learning. Co-creating knowledge with students provides an excellent foundation for all students because it permits cultural infusion in the process and disrupts the dominant culture. In the guide *Learner Involvement in the Co-creation of Teaching and Learning*, authors Konings et al. suggest that co-creating affects three levels:

1. the psychosocial learning environment

2. motivation and metacognition

3. educational design quality

They also designed the *Framework of Stakeholder Involvement* in co-creation, demonstrating the direct effects of co-creation on all stakeholders involved in restructuring education. You can adopt this as guidance to clarify your roles and responsibilities in a co-creating environment or as a guide for implementing collaborative strategies.

In 1994, Barry Fraser called the relationship between teachers and students the "psychosocial learning environment." The relationship between a student's psychological development and their interaction with the social environment is typically described using a combination of the words for those concepts, ending up with "psychosocial." This connection, also known as the student-environment relationship, has a significant impact on how motivated students are to participate in any given learning environment. Empowerment in a psychosocial learning environment significantly impacts inclusive learning, where students' emotions, ideas, interests, and abilities can be appropriately addressed and fostered.

Furthermore, students and teachers are more likely to improve their communication skills and attitudes toward collaboration and problem-solving in a co-creating environment. Communication is a critical component of shifting a classroom that does not already use co-creation as an inclusive strategy.

A student's motivation in all areas of life often directly relates to how well they perform in school and participate in successful learning. Students feel more motivated when they are confident in their abilities. Educator and author Ken Bain provides a list of strategies teachers might use to motivate their students, including:

- Pique your students' curiosity.

- Connect with them socially.

- Contextualize information.

- Develop meaningful assessments to reinforce what students learned.

- Set achievable and realistic goals for you and your students.

- Fairly evaluate students' work.

- Communicate their results with constructive feedback.

You must be willing to receive criticism and encourage students to take part in the process. Teachers may increase student motivation by meeting them where they are, providing access to content in modes that students prefer or can access, and offering positive feedback.

Overall, learners' metacognition, the awareness or analysis of one's own learning or thinking processes, involves actively monitoring, controlling, and assessing one's cognitive processes such as problem-solving and decision-making. Metacognitive strategies help individuals become more aware and better able to regulate their thoughts, feelings, and behaviors. It enhances their ability to problem-solve, evaluate ambiguous or complex scenarios and outcomes, and modify their learning skills based on their prior knowledge. Through metacognition, students can select the cognitive strategy that will most effectively assist them in achieving a personal objective.

Co-creation results in a successful, engaging curriculum while simultaneously enhancing curriculum design quality, depth of knowledge, and the perspectives of key stakeholders. This should be a top priority when designing inclusive classrooms, as the objective is to provide all students with a quality education. This approach differs from teacher-led design, where students have minimal input. A study by Brooman, Darwent, and Pimor found that when educators actively listen to students' voices, it boosts student performance, perceptions, and attendance. In the new hybrid culture of learning, this may also be a solution to mitigate the drop in student attendance.

As the world becomes more diverse, especially in the US, we all benefit by moving toward this approach to ensure that learning spaces capitalize on students' preexisting knowledge. This practice empowers students and yields the best results in knowledge retention and application to everyday life. As you think about collaborating with your students, consider your answers to the following questions:

- How have I historically collaborated with my students in the entire learning process?

- Do students have a choice and a voice in the classroom?

- Are they engaged with the current materials?

- What would be a desirable outcome for co-creating knowledge?

- What is my current classroom dynamic?

- Do I dominate the process, or do I facilitate it?

WHAT YOU CAN DO TOMORROW

Schools are not the only spaces where this occurs, but they are one of the most important ones for young people to develop their moral and social skills. Society entrusts you, as a teacher, with a critical role to offer students opportunities for conversations and interactions. Teri Dary and Terry Pickeral highlight the importance of creating a sustainable school culture where students develop such skills. They emphasize that teachers' capacity for self-reflection, commitment to prioritizing respect and care, and aptitude for drawing out students' moral vitality and knowledge are all essential to their success.

You can create inclusive classrooms and larger communities of practice that support students' emotional well-being by co-creating knowledge between teachers and students. Teachers must view themselves as learners and not let power dynamics impede inclusivity. We can teach students to take charge of their learning while we facilitate the process. Here are a few ideas to help you get started right away.

- **Identify the gaps by referencing your curriculum map.** For each course you teach, determine the areas where students already have collaboration opportunities, and then think about the gaps in the curriculum where you can broaden their involvement. By co-creating knowledge, you are showing students that you are learning with them. Start watching and working to find areas where you can foster inclusive, diverse thought. Ask your students to join you in identifying missing pieces in the curriculum to create experiences where everyone feels more involved and invested in the process and develops a sense of belonging. If your curriculum is generally prescribed, you can interject questions that connect to the observed gaps.

- **Ask students to list their preferred topics.** Although this varies by subject, allowing students a choice and inviting them to be a part of learning decisions empowers them and makes their school experience more inclusive and engaging. It also teaches them skills they can use beyond the classroom.

- **Plant metacognitive seeds.** Provide questions to guide students in practicing metacognition strategies. You can print this list, share it electronically, or create your own and distribute it to students.

  ▸ What do I need to do to understand this concept?

- How can I break down this task into smaller, more manageable steps?
- What strategies can I use to help me learn this material more effectively?
- What resources do I have available to help me learn this material?
- What am I already doing well in this area?
- How can I modify my learning approach to better understand this concept?
- What questions do I need to ask to make sure I understand this concept?
- What are the most important things for me to focus on to learn this material?
- What is the most effective way for me to remember and recall this material?
- How can I monitor my progress to stay on track?
- What key elements of this topic do I need to understand?
- How can I apply this knowledge to other areas of my learning?
- What tips can I use to better retain this information?
- What mistakes am I making that are preventing me from understanding this material?
- What strategies can I use to stay motivated to learn this material?

- **Create a system to integrate student feedback.**
Students love it when teachers listen to them and
consider their feedback. Feedback can make or
break the teaching experience. You can build in
ways for students to periodically share feedback
(directly or anonymously) about the classroom
content and activities, learning styles, resources,
and accessibility. Ideas include engaging students
in group discussions where they share ideas, use
anonymous surveys or questionnaires, participate
in student-led conferences, and utilize digital platforms such as Google Classroom or Edmodo to
post feedback. When you solicit student feedback,
you are co-creating information that you can use to
serve your students better. Chat with small groups
and meet with individuals to check in on what's
working. During study halls and lunch, you can
organize food-for-thought sessions for feedback on
how the class is going. Make sure you keep track
of the comments.

- **Implement a start, stop, and continue suggestion box.** Distribute a list of the semester's planned
topics, learning resources, and materials. Make
sure to include two to three sentences summarizing
each item. Then create a digital or physical suggestion box with three labeled sections for students to
add ideas. Allow students to work collaboratively
so they can make joint decisions with their classmates, based on the classroom demographics, so
that everyone feels included in the decision-making.

Allocate time for students to write down their ideas; if you are using a shared cloud document, give students time to begin typing their ideas during the classroom activity. If you are using a paper document, have students write their suggestions on separate pieces of paper and drop them in a suggestion box. Finally, analyze their suggestions and implement the feedback that will be beneficial to all. Student feedback not only helps us teach, but it also benefits everyone. It demonstrates that we value their ideas and that their opinions are central to our actions.

A BLUEPRINT FOR FULL IMPLEMENTATION

STEP 1: Know and understand your students.

Co-creation of knowledge calls for an understanding of your student population. Identify students who are already thriving and those who need extra help or accommodation. Establish a rapport with each student so you can better understand them. This may be challenging in bigger classrooms, so you may need to find creative ways to capture important information about your students to better understand them and their cultures, languages, and preferred modes of learning. Gain student trust by starting small and increasing involvement over time. Remember that you will continue to learn more about your students over the semester and year, and let relationships grow organically.

Consider using activities to get to know your students throughout the year. A quick and fun example you can use for different age groups is to assign creative writing or speaking about themselves and what they like. Start by modeling the process, such as a list of "I am" statements. Then read it aloud so they can get to know you a little bit more. See the following example.

- I was born in Rwanda, the land of a thousand hills.

- I was raised in Uganda, the Pearl of Africa.

- I am the firstborn child, the sibling who must set an example.

- I love nature; it brings me a sense of peace and calm.

- I am a fashionista; I love that fabrics and colors create beautiful, wearable art.

- I am an educator; one of the best gifts the world has ever seen.

- I am supportive and loving. I love putting a smile on my loved ones' faces.

- I am talented; singing and dancing are how I boost my mood when I feel low.

- I like to cook, especially Ugandan foods. We have one of the world's best diets.

- I am Black excellence; I take pride in the fact that I am my ancestors' wildest dream.

- I am resilient; I never give up, and I continue to reach for my dreams.

- I am strong. But also understand that it is okay to not be strong sometimes.

- I am loved. I surround myself with people who extend love and kindness to others.

STEP 2: Prioritize collaboration.

As educators, we do much of the heavy work independently, but it is also essential to consider students as resources. Generally, most teachers are required to follow a particular curriculum, but the curriculum becomes stronger when it is built collaboratively. Fill content gaps by adding opportunities that are helpful for diverse student populations—this is where student-teacher partnerships can help. Collaborate with students by creating group projects that spark their interests and build opportunities to learn from each other. You, too, will learn from their collaborations, and this will help you gather additional valuable feedback.

STEP 3: Set expectations.

This valuable step cultivates an inclusive teaching environment because it helps clarify the balance between students' individual efforts and the classroom's collective efforts. I highly encourage you and your students to work together to develop expectations as early in the school year as possible.

Determine the aspects of teaching that are absolutely nonnegotiable for you. Plan ahead to either facilitate a class discussion about expectations or to present your concept and allow the students to modify it. Ask the students working in small groups to reflect on previous learning contexts. What kinds of educational environments were most beneficial and successful? What aspects of those environments did they like or dislike? How can you all collaboratively improve their experiences based on their commentary? Encourage your students to write lists of expectations for the class based on the conversations that have taken place so far. Gather and compile the lists. Make necessary changes to them, and communicate the revised versions throughout the classroom to get everyone's feedback. When everyone has had a chance to give feedback and gain understanding, then include the criteria in your curriculum. Check in with the students during the school year to see if the expectations are still reasonable, and adjust them as necessary.

STEP 4: Put your students at the center of the curriculum.

Traditional curricula are predominantly Eurocentric and exclude culturally and linguistically diverse (or racialized) students' experiences, cultures, and languages. Co-creation allows for diversifying materials based on your students' needs and makes room for social justice in their learning.

Listen to your students: how they speak, what motivates them, their cultural practices, and their unique traditions. Encourage them to constructively contribute to curriculum development and collaboratively create solutions to problems. Establish relationships with them, their parents/guardians, and the community. Ensure that your curriculum, classroom activities, and assessments include all students, based on what you have learned about them and their community.

STEP 5: Amplify student voices.

To effectively amplify student voices, incorporate their multicultural backgrounds into the curriculum. Listen to them; they can speak for themselves. This approach aligns with what Sarah Lambert, a researcher in open education, defines as sociocultural diversity in the curriculum, which, in addition to representational justice, is the autonomy of marginalized individuals and groups to speak for themselves.

Engage students in natural, critical conversations and consider their well-being beyond academic performance. This will help you advocate for them and authentically amplify their voices because you will better understand their stories. Include them in decision-making, such as by asking them to vote on best practices or simple tasks like compiling a classroom-appropriate playlist for break-time music.

STEP 6: Make it safe for students to speak up.

If students resist participating in an activity, communicate with them about their concerns in ways that help them feel comfortable. Start involving students in the curriculum early on to develop their confidence in contributing. Consider innovative alternatives to in-person discussions about the course. For example, you can ask students to submit anonymous course feedback so they have more choice and control over how they communicate with you. See Hack 1 for ideas on making students comfortable.

STEP 7: Let students coach their classmates.

Students are more likely to listen to and relate to their peers, so you can leverage the skills of students who are interested in serving as leaders and those who are eager to share their learning. Excite students about leadership by incentivizing it. For instance, grant them autonomy over a particular lesson or allow them to select the app of the day or the theme song for the day. Choose a rotation system so all students can participate in demonstrating their leadership abilities. You could order them alphabetically, by birthday, or on a volunteer basis. You can also develop student leadership through group collaboration, with specific student groups serving as mentors to their peers in areas such as technology, organization, research, and presentations. This system allows students to learn from one another while also allowing you to sit back and facilitate their experience.

STEP 8: Celebrate your students' progress.

Acknowledging student efforts is an important incentive for them to demonstrate their knowledge, skills, creativity, and ideas. Students are more likely to stay engaged if their efforts are "seen," as this shows that you have high expectations for them. By holding all students accountable for producing high-quality work and recognizing their achievements, teachers demonstrate their genuine concern for their students' welfare.

Consider a student spotlight weekly, biweekly, or monthly. Throw a class party at the end of the year to recognize everyone's hard work, and involve parents and the community in celebrating student achievements. You may even want to create gamified digital communities in which students can track their progress and compete in healthy ways. For example, in language classrooms, consider applications like Duolingo, Memrise, LinguaLift, and Rosetta Stone for gamifying and celebrating student milestones. My personal favorite is Memrise, a solid app for students to improve their vocabulary while having fun.

OVERCOMING PUSHBACK

At any grade level, you might encounter opposition about co-creating knowledge, and it might come from the administration, other teachers, or parents. The key is to understand that your priority is your students and stand firm in your decision to transform their student experiences positively. As you attempt and even fail, obstacles will present themselves, but your efforts will not be wasted. Your students will have a better learning experience. Here's how to address common questions.

Students should not have that much power in your classroom. Believing that students will overtake the learning experience due to power dynamics is problematic because the alternative is that students are excluded from the process. Engaging students and collaborating with them does not take away from your role as a teacher. Instead, it breaks down barriers and pulls in students— which can transform their perspectives on learning. It yields positive outcomes for both teachers and students.

Co-creating with students is like having "too many cooks in the kitchen" and will likely lead to conflict. On the contrary, co-creating is necessary and reflects how the real world functions. When classes co-create knowledge, teachers and students constantly work to improve their attitudes, communication, partnerships, and conflict management abilities. It also allows them to collaborate on common goals and create win-win situations. Students benefit from inclusive teaching, which improves their academic performance.

The curriculum does not provide sufficient time for co-creating knowledge with students. This is a legitimate concern, but there are a few workarounds. Instead of a big change like a new curriculum, consider starting with small projects related to your work, building on existing collaborative opportunities with your students, and then adjusting accordingly. This will prevent you from having to reinvent the wheel or spend additional time creating the "perfect" environment for co-creation. It also facilitates co-creation and encourages students to become active contributors. You can collaborate with other teachers who are also implementing co-creation in their classrooms to share experiences and ideas, learn from each other's efforts, and come up with solutions to any problems that arise. As teachers, we must always be creative with what we are already doing to enhance the learning and teaching experience. Co-creation requires time, so it is best to begin with a small-scale implementation and expand as you gain experience.

I feel like my expertise gives me the authority to make executive judgments about the curriculum. Some teachers worry that restructuring their current pedagogical practices threatens their authority. Changing traditional hierarchical structures can be challenging, especially if you can't deconstruct them with other teachers and leaders who share a common goal. More specifically, you can use your expertise to provide guidance and structure to the co-creation process while still allowing students to have ownership and take the initiative in the process. For example, you can provide students with a framework and criteria for their project and then guide them in identifying resources and developing project ideas that meet the criteria. Help to facilitate collaboration among students as they brainstorm and create their projects.

THE HACK IN ACTION

Ms. Alissa Irvin, a Black teacher and scholar in curriculum and instruction, has an array of experience and expertise. Understanding her background is critical to understanding how her experience shaped her role as a co-creator with her students. She currently teaches undergraduate students at a four-year higher education institution in the Midwest. She has also taught third and fourth graders in an "alternative" school in southwest Ohio. In higher education, she has taught courses such as Social Justice, School, and Society; Principles in Teaching Literature to Children and Youth; and Introduction to African American Studies. In her primary grade teaching, she taught third and fourth graders the core curriculum classes such as social studies, reading, and math. Irvin taught in school-based settings for seven years and, nontraditionally, in community spaces, after-school programs, and homes through youth and family care positions for fifteen years.

Irvin uses incredible strategies to infuse the co-creation of knowledge in her classroom. Given who she is and her experiences, her ideal culturally inclusive space is one where Black children can learn about themselves and one another through a diasporic lens: a way of looking at the world through an understanding of the relationship between displacement, identity, and culture. It is an analytical tool that helps to shed light on the unique experiences of diaspora communities: the ways they connect to their homeland and how their home countries and the countries they reside in represent them.

Cultural inclusivity is primarily rooted in self-knowledge and expands this understanding globally. When Black children are able to keenly know who they are and feel safe and affirmed in this knowledge, as well as know their contributions to society, they can situate themselves as global citizens. Irvin firmly believes that creating an inclusive space for all cultures requires integrating authentic and purposeful cultural pedagogical practices rather than simply supplementing them.

As a Black woman educator, Irvin asserts that her mothering as a Black woman is a political role that influences, if not governs, her approach to cultural inclusivity. She actively listens to her students and develops lessons and pedagogy that not only respect but intentionally incorporate their languages and cultural norms. In addition, she fosters a close-knit classroom community by having all students sit together and facilitating a brave space where they can be themselves while also encouraging and bolstering one another's growth in understanding of each other. This further demonstrates that taking action and investing in social justice requires an awareness of the world around us and a critical understanding of the ways in which our respective worlds intersect and influence one another.

She challenges her students to examine their positionality: how differences in social position and power shape identities and access to society. Positionality shapes their interactions with the world—connecting them back to their languages, cultures, and other aspects of who they are, how they view themselves, and how society portrays them. As a result, her approach has enabled her and her students to see each other both literally and figuratively, which is essential for creating spaces for critical thinking about language and culture. Irvin firmly believes that names are important as an entry point to the discussion of language and culture, as they are typically a reflection of these two areas that are closely tied to our identities, allowing students to engage in the learning and sharing in a more intimate and meaningful manner. She is intentional about asking students' names, their pronunciations, and their meanings, and she incorporates those details into her practice.

For example, she facilitates class discussions in various formats and encourages her students to reflect critically on and articulate their linguistic assumptions and knowledge. To help students grasp the fundamentals, she leads them through in-depth discussions in smaller groups and asks them theoretically grounded, guided questions. She selects relevant media that challenge students' understanding of language and culture and how they both inform our individual belief systems. Examples include tweets, Facebook posts, and blog posts that all touch on language and culture in some way; court cases where linguistic and cultural biases played a role in rulings; and pictures in books and old newspapers that present the same events from different people's points of view and draw different conclusions about them.

Overall, Irvin attributes co-creating knowledge as a strategy for constructing a culturally inclusive environment in which students connect ideas driven by abstract thoughts about a topic that require them to think through sense-making as a small group or community from each of their perspectives. Often, this method does not intend to develop an answer as much as it supports collective community consideration for moving forward and learning how this would operate in society, which brings in the practice of connecting classes to societal realities. How the classroom discourse shows up in the real world is critical for students to apply the discussion or content and understand how its approach matters.

Irvin helps students connect to societal realities. She encourages students to put their knowledge to use in ways that broadly and purposefully take communities into account. She says that teachers can decrease the gap between school and home by drawing on the knowledge and skills that students acquire in their families and communities. This knowledge has been an invaluable resource for her classes, as valuing and incorporating native languages and cultures has greatly increased students' abilities to apply what they have learned. It also allows students from outside the culture and language to appreciate cultures other than their own, which holds the potential to foster a sense of community among students.

Irvin regularly faces pushback about her work and how she approaches teaching. She expects it and navigates it accordingly. From her experience, it is clear that traditional teaching methods have both advantages and disadvantages. They privilege dominant groups while perpetuating a marginalized attitude toward racialized groups. She is deliberate in her rejection, resistance, and disruption of these preexisting constraints. She introduces her classes with an awareness that pushback is likely, as she understands the discomfort that accompanies this topic. She also grounds ideas and thoughts in additional core materials that offer perspectives otherwise deemed unimportant or disregarded altogether. The voices she introduces into the teaching are voices that have previously been excluded from traditional curricula. Irvin's inclusion of her students' cultures and languages does not begin and end with them but instead centers on them as a pedagogical strategy.

Traditional pedagogical approaches impede students' capacities to conceive new educational techniques. Teachers can address this issue. It is difficult for students to comprehend their position as stakeholders in the co-creation process since they are not consistently exposed to the complete process. If applied correctly, co-creation can provide useful ideas from both the teacher and student perspectives, contributing to the development of more inclusive, democratic learning settings that disrupt existing hierarchies. It can improve instructional design, provide high-quality materials, and give instructors and students additional opportunities to express themselves and receive feedback.

As the world, and the United States in particular, grows increasingly diverse, it's time to embrace co-creation to ensure that classroom environments maximize previous knowledge and enhance learning. According to studies on successful educational practices, co-creating knowledge empowers students and produces the greatest outcomes in information retention and everyday application. Consider how you have engaged and included your students throughout the learning process in the past as you plan future interactions with them. Imagine the possible outcomes of teacher-student cooperation for you and your students. Focus on facilitating the process and allowing students to assume a more direct and proactive part in their learning experience. It will boost the quality and efficacy of classroom discussions.

EMPLOY TRANSLANGUAGING METHODS

Use Students' Home Languages and Cultures as a Resource

Before students can use their language as a critical resource to build new skills, they must be able to view their language as intellectually valuable.
— April Baker-Bell, transdisciplinary teacher and activist

THE PROBLEM: EDUCATION PROGRAMS DO NOT EQUIP TEACHERS WITH THE NECESSARY TOOLS

It is our responsibility as educators to meet our students where they are and provide them with the necessary tools for success without lowering our expectations.

Racialized students in the US experience overlapping forms of academic, linguistic, and racial prejudice. According to the National Center for Education Statistics, in the 2017–18 school year, 79 percent of public school teachers were White and non-Hispanic, which explains the lack of representation of racialized teachers in classrooms. As a result, thousands of Black, Latinx, and Indigenous students attend schools where there are no same-race teachers or where they are taught by teachers from different ethnic backgrounds. Most teachers likely have limited knowledge about their students' histories and cultures.

Naturally, we know more about our own communities. The lack of multicultural representation in schools or the curriculum has been studied for decades, but the gap between theory and practice persists.

Pierre Bourdieu extended a theory of linguistic exchange that said, in effect, "The properties of the market (jobs, institutions, assessment tools, technologies) determine the value of the linguistic products. Some 'products' hold a higher value than others." This is a prime example of the colonial, racist logic that fuels raciolinguistic ideologies, even in education. When we do not value students' diverse languages, it clearly shows, and they can internalize that. Evidently, we, as educators, must work on bridging the gap between literature and practice, creating opportunities for better academic experiences and ending unnecessary academic setbacks for both teachers and students.

Traditional instruction is aimed toward mainstream students, and teachers sometimes lack the skills required to provide language-minority students access to the English curriculum. This also opens up additional opportunities for students who are monolingual and speak standard English, while linguistically diverse students take on unfair responsibilities to "assimilate" or "blend in." Research shows us that monolingual, English-speaking instructors often enable White, English-dominant students to disrupt, extend, and dominate learning processes. In contrast, bilingual, two-way immersion teachers more often strive to balance students' positions and authority, which nurtures linguistic diversity.

Nelson Flores and Ofelia García published "A Critical Review of Bilingual Education in the United States," and in it, they remind us of two goals of bilingual education that emerged in the post–civil rights era: 1) for the programs to improve the self-esteem of linguistically and culturally diverse students (LCDS) by instilling confidence, and 2) for the programs to address the multilingualism of LCDS by giving them a solid foundation in their first language.

Transitional bilingual education (TBE) makes up most bilingual education programs in the United States. Although TBE programs can serve non-English language groups, most serve Spanish-speaking students. This remains a challenge because student demographics are rapidly changing, and schools can't account for many languages. The extent of diverse language representation in US bilingual education varies by state and district.

Generally, the most commonly taught language in bilingual education is Spanish. According to the US Department of Education, in the 2016–17 school year, most bilingual programs utilized Spanish (83 percent), followed by French (7 percent), Chinese (3 percent), Vietnamese (2 percent), and Arabic (1 percent).

However, African/Black languages are barely offered, even though Black immigrants continue to increase in schools. This is a challenge for students needing linguistic resources and teaching strategies that will nurture their home and school languages. Research frequently records contradictions between policy and reality. Although bilingual programs promise students and parents that they will nurture their home languages, many teachers employ "assimilative" practices, prioritizing standard English over other languages to maintain monolingual ideologies.

Another challenge lies in using programs built through categorization, although we have varying capabilities among students. For example, Dual Language Education is another form of Bilingual Education, divided into three types of dual language programs: immersion programs, two-way immersion programs, and developmental or dual language programs in languages other than English. The goal is to develop bilingualism.

> *Translanguaging is a process in which a student draws on multiple languages to express themselves or to enhance their communication.*

It can be challenging for most racialized students with underrepresented languages to thrive in bilingual programs. Multilingual learners benefit more when encouraged to use their knowledge in one language to enhance their proficiency in another language, which calls for educators to embrace and capitalize on students' linguistic diversity and cultural and experiential knowledge.

Overall standard curricula and schools often underappreciate or don't acknowledge the depth of cultural knowledge and values that culturally diverse students possess. Researchers urge teachers to engage with the life experiences of multicultural students in academic and social settings by appreciating the rich cultural diversity these students bring to the classroom and gaining an understanding of it.

THE HACK: EMPLOY TRANSLANGUAGING METHODS

Scholars emphasize the significance of understanding culturally and linguistically diverse student populations. It is critical that educators acknowledge the value that students' languages bring and be intentional about how we influence student perceptions regarding their linguistics. When we tap into *translanguaging*, a process in which a student draws on multiple languages to express themselves or to enhance their communication, we can ensure that each multilingual student uses and honors their full linguistic repertoire.

What does translanguaging look like in the classroom? Teachers use a holistic approach, taking into account all students' linguistic and cognitive abilities to make meaning or comprehend the classroom material being taught in a language different from theirs. Integrating anti-racist, asset-based, and critical language pedagogy (such as translanguaging) would put teachers in a better position to disrupt current practices that perpetuate linguistic injustices.

Translanguaging can provide students with access to classroom content, enhance participation and engagement with the curriculum, help build strong relationships between students and their teachers, and support students in representing their linguistic diversity. It also challenges the "two solitudes" method of bilingualism, suggesting that multilingual speakers transfer between languages instead of using their full linguistic repertoires such as registers, styles, dialects, and accents.

Others point out the political and disruptive nature of translanguaging, revealing how it enables linguistically minoritized students to have opportunities to critique and push against monoglossic ideologies. Teachers must shift toward a translingual approach that views linguistic diversity as a resource for meaning-making in writing, speaking, reading, and listening rather than a deficit or hindrance. The Bell Foundation contends that encouraging bilingual, multilingual, and culturally diverse students to use their entire linguistic repertoire empowers them and helps them utilize their full learning potential.

Teachers can develop a supportive attitude toward multilingualism, which numerous experts and activists continuously advocate as the ideal. Tove Skutnabb-Kangas and others criticized what they viewed as linguicism and created the term "linguistic human rights." According to Shawn Levy et al., when schools view a student's first language negatively, those students may feel less included. Jean Conteh states that valuing multilingualism and linguistic diversity in classrooms helps racialized students succeed. Students can show up as their whole selves, integrate their home languages and cultures, and experience an improved learning experience when teachers value their languages. In research published by Ofelia García, Susana Ibarra Johnson, and Kate Seltzer, they outlined four objectives for the thoughtful inclusion of translanguaging in the classroom:

1. Allowing students to practice their language skills in academic settings

2. Allowing multilingual students and different modes of knowing

3. Fostering students' socioemotional development and bilingual identities

4. Assisting students in understanding difficult texts and subject matter

Planning and gathering the necessary resources can achieve these goals in your classroom. When teachers implement translanguaging strategies, they enable students to feel comfortable and engaged in otherwise difficult and isolating learning environments. It also allows students to share their language and subject-matter knowledge with their classmates. Teachers who provide multilingual learning opportunities for their students cultivate a classroom environment where each student works not only within their developmental level—but also within their comfort zone.

This fosters cross-cultural communication in the classroom and enhances student participation and self-esteem. Ask yourself questions regarding the four goals that García, Johnson, and Seltzer proposed, such as:

1. How am I already providing opportunities for students to develop linguistic skills in academic contexts?

2. Have I created space for my multilingual students and their diverse ways of knowing?

3. How do I support my bilingual and multilingual students' identities and their socioemotional development?

4. How do I plan on supporting my students as they engage with and comprehend complex materials?

As you reflect on your responses, consider the core components of teachers' translanguaging pedagogy in Image 3.1.

COMPONENT	APPLICATION	EXAMPLES
STANCE	Adopt the belief that it's essential to tap into your students' varied linguistic practices.	Not prioritizing one language over the other(s).
DESIGN	Use students' language practices to guide instructional design, units, lesson plans, and assessments.	Do this when introducing new concepts and incorporating different spellings and pronunciations.
SHIFT	Be flexible and openly alter your instructional plan based on student input, performance, and understanding.	Not translating everything encourages students to use their home languages in the same language or cultural small groups.

Image 3.1: Core components of translanguaging pedagogy.

For Black students specifically, I propose the Afrolinguistic capital framework—which situates African and African descendants' linguistic practices as valuable, necessary, and sufficient. Bourdieu's concept of capital suggests that there are different forms of capital, not just economic capital in the real sense but also cultural capital, such as knowledge, skills, other cultural acquisitions, symbolic capital, and more. Regarding linguistic capital, Bourdieu states that different speakers possess different quantities of it. Specifically, it refers to the capacity in which they can manipulate expressions for a "market" (such as an institution or job). Bourdieu's theory of practice and overall work on language and power tended to favor dominant European languages such as French and English. His conceptualization of linguistic capital and the linguistic marketplace contributed to exclusive racist rhetoric that devalues racialized languages even here in the US to this day. Hence the need for the raciolinguistic perspective and application of frameworks such as Afrolinguistic capital to counter these harmful ideologies. In this case, the framework would aid educators in applying translanguaging methods for Black students. Cultural capital is not only limited to an individual but should extend to families and larger groups of people. Teachers should adopt the same attitudes toward Black students to disrupt language-based discrimination and the stigmatization of their diverse linguistic expression.

WHAT YOU CAN DO TOMORROW

The purpose of implementing translanguaging methods is to stimulate and facilitate the use of a student's holistic linguistic repertoire. As students become more acclimated to translanguaging, it becomes more natural for both students and teachers. Educators can apply the same strategies to "mainstream" classes. Here are ideas you can put into practice right away.

- **Use equivalents and cognates.** Create glossaries to allow your bilingual and multilingual students to make meaning in diverse ways and personalize their learning experience. It also adds value to languages historically deemed less valuable in the academic setting. Teachers can use glossaries in language arts and other subjects, especially when introducing new concepts. The objective is to give students various linguistic conceptualization strategies so they can build on their prior knowledge. In some languages, such as Spanish and English, words have equivalents (the same meaning) in both languages. This similarity provides a preexisting translation foundation for students learning the other language.

  For example, ask students to complete an assigned classroom reading. As students read their texts, ask them to identify five to ten cognates and write them down. Cognates are words that share a similar meaning, spelling, and pronunciation in different languages. Arrange students in groups and have them share the words they found to see if any of them are similar. Ask them to compare the words, cross out duplicates, and then compile their findings into a single table, with one side in English and the other in a different language. Read or have students read them aloud to the class. Discuss the similarities and differences in the spelling and pronunciation of the cognates.

- **Incorporate different spellings and pronunciations.** This is a unique way to support diverse linguistic practices and also tap into students' holistic language repertoires. A great example is to encourage Black students to spell and pronounce African American Language (AAL) and standard American English when teaching a new concept or collaborating on activities. See Appendix B.1 for an activity example for a high school classroom that involves conducting a research project to address a social problem.

- **Stop translating everything.** Even if you are fluent in another language that you share with some of your students, it is best not to translate everything. Researchers and practitioners of translanguaging methods warn that it is not helpful, or sustainable, to translate everything for students. Empower them by providing the necessary resources, such as dictionaries and word glossaries. Allow them to have more autonomy in their learning process and connect the dots independently.

- **Encourage students to use their home languages in the same small groups arranged by language or culture.** You can create plenty of opportunities in the classroom for students to use their home languages. Dividing them into small groups with others who share a language or culture can bring them closer and tap into their holistic linguistic abilities as they work together.

  If possible, group students so they can work with language partners on larger projects. Encourage students to use their native languages to work on and present their final projects. They can conduct their research by navigating through divided topics or themes in their small groups and taking notes in several languages. This is a great way to build a welcoming community that nurtures students' learning. You can reference a related activity in Appendix B.2.

- **Prioritize various languages equally.** Although the US does not have an official language at the federal level, English continues to dominate the majority of the schooling system and structures in place, although there are at least three hundred other languages spoken in the country. This is a clear reflection of our society—language ideologies and hierarchies. We must treat all languages equally and avoid perpetuating the linguistic disparity in educational settings and beyond. The book *Words and Actions: Teaching Languages Through the Lens of Social Justice* offers language teachers a practical framework for social justice-focused pedagogy as well as links to additional resources. Also consider the following idea starters:

  ▸ Utilize multiple languages in the classroom. Teachers can create a multilanguage classroom by incorporating different languages into the instruction, activities, and assessments.

  ▸ Encourage students to share their language and culture. Allow students to present in their native language and introduce their culture to the class.

▸ Create a classroom environment that is supportive and accepting of all languages.

▸ Encourage students to respect and appreciate the diversity of languages in the classroom.

▸ Provide resources for all languages. Make sure all students have access to resources in their native language.

▸ Emphasize the importance of communication. Focus on the ability to communicate and understand multiple languages instead of proficiency in one language.

▸ Use language-neutral activities. Design activities that do not rely on one particular language.

▸ Celebrate language diversity. Promote language-rich activities and celebrate the diverse languages in the classroom.

- **Develop background with the preview-view-review strategy.** David and Yvonne Freeman present this method, which employs both the new language and the student's native language to establish context, strengthen the foundation for reading texts, and introduce new concepts. There are three essential components:

  Preview the materials in the home language. This stage focuses on making connections, coming up with ideas, and talking about what students already know about the subject.

  View the materials in the new language and make connections with the students' home language preview. Use this strategy when delivering content to the students in their "new" language. At this stage, the main takeaway is that students can make strong links between what they know in their native language and what they are learning in the target language.

Review the materials in the home language and switch back to the new language. This stage is primarily concerned with developing critical arguments or grappling with the learned content, as well as summarizing and analyzing the text or topic in the native language and through translanguaging. This stage gives students the opportunity to explain and discuss items in English, which enhances their comprehension of the topic.

- **Draw from the collective cultural wealth of students.** For example, the Black community includes many nuances, including colonial history, enslavement, immigration, and other events that have significantly influenced the construction of different languages and cultures of Africans and African descendants. To understand Black students and the rich diversity within their communities (such as African, Caribbean, and other immigrants), you must know both the influences and the overall impact.

  Respect the collective cultural wealth that speakers of Pan-African languages possess both personally and collectively on a global level. It is a call for respect, integration, and even the equitable distribution of power rather than an invitation to generalize or stereotype Africans and people of African descent and their customs. Avoid making assumptions about what students know or don't know. Instead, involve them in your investigation into their histories or backgrounds. Let them learn and teach alongside you.

- **Acknowledge and promote diverse Pan-African linguistic practices.** The Afrolinguistic capital framework considers all Pan-African linguistic skills (accents, styles, dialects, and language variations) as valuable capital. It views multilingualism as an asset and a resource. In that sense, this aspect of the framework suggests that you address preconceived notions and negative attitudes toward Pan-African linguistic practices and invest in authentic representation in different spaces and contexts.

  The entire world borrows from and is influenced by Black culture and language—continuously adding new Black language vocabulary to the Urban Dictionary. There is a long history of society using and praising Black culture and language when it is beneficial or "cool," usually at the expense of Black people because they do not reap the benefits of such exploitation. You can be a part of the change.

  Welcome African, Caribbean, or African American accents of your students, and do not assume that their accents mean they have low English proficiency. Be understanding when students who are new to the US and barely speak English attempt to articulate or pronounce words that may require extra time to understand. Work hard to help them feel comfortable about their accents. Never "dumb down" or speak slowly when speaking to them. Instead, encourage them to ask questions or seek assistance. Converse with them as you would anyone. Experience is the best teacher, so don't automatically assume that someone can't understand you just because you speak at a different pace. People understand more than they can express, especially when they are multilingual, because their brain has to process a lot more information. The part of the brain that understands language is physically different than the part that creates it.

- **Catch yourself before you generalize about students.** Every student is linguistically unique, so be aware of your assumptions and stop yourself before you express them. For example, it's unfortunately common for teachers to presume that all Black immigrants speak English with an accent, are not native English speakers, or are expected to speak a certain way because they are not American.

- **Acknowledge that preexisting racial and linguistic categories cannot fully account for all ethnoracial groups' practices.** Due to their distinct histories, experiences, and ongoing language and identity reconstruction, Africans and people of African descent have limitless linguistic potential, and their linguistic practices will continue to evolve. As a result, no number of categories will ever "fit" all ethnoracial groups. As educators, we must reconsider how the fluidity of racial identification prompts us to question systems of racial categorization in order to shift our collective thinking about language and race. This aspect of the Afrolinguistic capital framework guides "perceiving subjects" (individuals who are aware of the complexities of race and racism and can recognize and interpret the racialized experiences of others) to reimagine the limits of naturalized categories in order to allow Pan-African linguistics to exist without limitations.

- **Advocate for linguistic freedom.** Incorporate practices that allow Africans and African descendants to exercise their linguistic freedom without modifying themselves to fit the "norm" (codeswitching). Baker-Bell states that schools devalue a Black child's language, which reflects how the world devalues their lives. On a countering note, the world deems White culture normal, neutral, and superior. As educators, we can demand linguistic justice, anti-racist pedagogy, the disruption of anti-Blackness, and the undoing of raciolinguistic ideologies. Integrating Pan-African languages into practices aligns with the linguistic freedom aspect of Afrolinguistic capital because it empowers Pan-African language speakers to not be afraid to be authentic in speaking their languages and even to explore learning new ones. Hold yourself and others accountable when racial and linguistic harm is perpetuated.

  For a classroom activity, create a virtual or physical "language news bulletin board" and keep up with hot topics about diverse languages in the US and internationally. You and your students can both contribute to this bulletin board throughout the school year—and highlight areas that the media usually does not focus on in order to raise awareness and normalize linguistic diversity.

- **Combat raciolinguistic ideologies.** Resist behaviors that foster racial ideologies. For example, recognize that racialized students' home languages already coincide with the linguistic information encoded in state standards (and other specialized requirements). Start constructing lessons and courses based on that existing knowledge and discard dichotomous framings of language where something is either "right" or "wrong" without allowing for shades of gray. Avoid exams and scales that incorrectly measure racialized students' literacy proficiency and move away from assimilative methods to learning and teaching by adding culturally inclusive pedagogies.

- **Apply the Raciolinguistics Theory of Change.** Treat all languages equally since they are legitimate and valuable. Create lessons, for example, that promote Django Paris's culturally inclusive pedagogy. Avoid harmful practices that have historically been portrayed as useful to racialized students (such as "correcting" accents and dialects). Instead, be deliberate in identifying deficit-based methods and practices, as well as in implementing solutions to alter teaching and learning in your classroom. Ensure your approach prioritizes student perspectives and experiences while involving students in all stages of lessons. Your classroom can be a model of anti-racist pedagogy with curricula designed to resolve conflicts between students' home and school languages and brave spaces for learning languages across all student populations, bringing students into embracing different cultures through literacy. As a direct result, culturally and linguistically diverse or racialized students will communicate in dominant languages while still asserting their linguistic diversity and social mobility.

- **Use the window or mirror strategy for deep and critical reading.** This reading, inspired by Teaching Tolerance, allows students to gain empathy and compassion for the lived experiences of others. It also encourages students to examine social, cultural, political, and historical settings. Get students thinking about whether a certain text serves as a "window" or a "mirror": how they can learn more about others or more about themselves. Design activities that will guide them through evaluating if the author, speaker, characters, or content align with their own experiences or provide insight into their peers of different identities. You can find the steps for the activity in Appendix B.3.

A BLUEPRINT FOR FULL IMPLEMENTATION

STEP 1: Promote respect for all learners.

View all classrooms as multicultural. Work toward respecting, valuing, and celebrating your own and students' unique strengths in creating equitable classroom communities. It helps to know and recognize the holidays of various cultural groups. If your school encourages celebrations, celebrate them all equally. You can use related activities to employ an intersectionality lens to examine and clarify how we differ and are similar to others on a local and global scale. Emphasize the need to learn the significance of the traditions and customs of our many cultures; history plays a huge role in our future. Identify, research, and incorporate each student's life experiences. Use the information you collect to plan curriculum or as a bank of knowledge and resources.

STEP 2: Utilize funds of knowledge.

All families possess a set of resources and knowledge that can be used to support their children's learning and development. Culturally and linguistically responsive research and pedagogical strategies improve students' sense of agency, motivation, and academic performance. Incorporating the knowledge they bring to the classroom opens opportunities to recognize and value their languages and cultures.

Curate materials and resources that reflect the cultural and ethnic diversity of our society and communities. Include generationally appropriate media and integrate technology that students are already using outside of the classroom into the curriculum (social media, podcasts, mobile devices, communication and collaboration platforms, and creative suites). Build lessons and projects that expand on students' passions and experiences outside of school and support their bilingual identities and socioemotional development. It benefits all students when you encourage them to dig deeper into their lives, homes, and communities so everyone can learn more about their histories as well as their current state. If you want to go further, you can ask them to document their reflections in journals—and use the journals in roundtable discussions to transfer knowledge with their peers.

STEP 3: Incorporate diverse language practices.

An inclusive classroom is more than just one that accepts students' different language habits; it integrates them into the learning. In a *Review of Education* article titled "Making Visible Awareness in Practice: Literacy Educators in Diverse Classrooms," Patriann Smith et al. recommend exposing pre-service teachers to different "ways of being and doing" for students with a variety of cultural backgrounds and languages, including variations of English. Even if this exposure wasn't part of your education, you can start now and integrate diverse linguistic and cultural considerations into lessons and activities. Look for ways to model this approach to new teachers.

Consider including culturally and linguistically diverse books, speakers, movies, and other materials to "hear" students' voices, support their representation, and foster a feeling of belonging. In bilingual education, you may want to construct a library that contains literature in several languages (for example, Black English, Jamaican and Haitian Creole, West African Pidgin, and Spanish). Create curricula that normalize diverse languages, denaturalize linguistic categorization, and dismantle ethnic prejudices. Denaturalizing linguistic categorization involves challenging assumptions and norms about language and how it is used, such as the idea that certain languages or dialects are superior to others. Instead, celebrate the uniqueness of different language varieties, rejecting the idea that language is fixed and static and instead embracing its dynamic and ever-evolving nature. Design activities that allow students who speak different dialects of English to read and write in the dialect of their choice. Such practices encourage students to reflect on the diversity in the classroom as well as how they and others perceive their ethnic, racial, and linguistic backgrounds.

STEP 4: Stay abreast of research on best practices.

When you actively seek resources and knowledge about best practices, it will help you to incorporate new, relevant pedagogy solutions and decrease the gap between theory and practice. You will tailor your pedagogical strategies to the needs of your students more effectively by continually developing your understanding of your students' backgrounds. Seek a greater awareness of students' language and cultural histories (such as colonialism and immigration), as well as their personal experiences, through interactions with other students, parents, and the community at large. Adopt an open-door policy for parents, allowing them to visit the classroom. You could engage them further by including them in their children's educational experiences. For example, design an activity where students and their parents lead a discussion around a theme (family life, holidays, staple foods), or have them choose a different point of interest. Consider using graphic organizers or having classroom conferences to check in with students and evaluate their progress.

STEP 5: Be the change you want to see.

For our students to see what's possible and follow your lead, they need to see you model it. Modeling practices that reflect what students need inside and outside of the classroom can transform how they view their world and imagine what kind of change they, too, can make in their lives and communities. Demonstrate vulnerability and transparency with your students. When you make mistakes or work through challenges in front of the class, it allows students to reflect on their shortcomings, questions they fear to ask, and their reservations—in real time. It makes you, the teacher, more accessible and creates a welcoming environment for all learners. Don't make jokes about students' accents or spelling because you never know how the student may interpret it—or if they are already dealing with linguistic insecurities or internalized linguistic ideologies. Instead, exemplify helpfulness, encouragement, and inclusivity.

STEP 6: Use graphic organizers.

Students use graphic organizers to integrate ideas and information. Some students are more receptive when familiar cultural artifacts—like music, art, and TV imagery—are included in their learning. Students who are more receptive to auditory and visual approaches than reading- or writing-based approaches may benefit by using graphic organizers to diversify learning methods in your classroom.

For example, use a KWL chart (Know-Want-Learned) (see Image 3.2) to gauge students' understanding and prime their knowledge at particular points of learning. They can organize their thoughts before doing research and keep track of their findings to reinforce what they already know and prompt them to decide where they want to concentrate their learning. Ask them what they already *know* about the topic at hand, what they *want* to know, and what they *learned* by researching a topic. This strategy is powerful because it also activates their funds of knowledge as they progress. See a sample lesson for a critical book review essay in Appendix B.4.

I KNOW	I WANT TO KNOW	I LEARNED

Image 3.2: The Know-Want-Learned (KWL) approach.

STEP 7: Be open to "walking an extra mile" to create equitable learning spaces.

Most teachers perpetuate problematic practices to some degree and continue to explicitly or blindly reproduce them. But awareness generates change, and it's okay to move forward from this point and begin to get comfortable having uncomfortable discussions about social change. Reflect on your positionality in the world and be as transparent as possible with students about your perspectives based on your positionality. Use tactics that allow students to have greater control over their academic and social lives by giving them more agency. Push your practices to better involve students in community-based research and service projects to foster the development of critical thinking skills.

STEP 8: Tie it all together with the three pillars of translanguaging.

Translanguaging emphasizes attitude, planning, and flexibility. When you believe that translanguaging is a valuable strategy in the classroom and use CLD students' home language practices as resources, it will naturally guide your approach. Plan activities, exercises, and tasks that allow students to use both languages. Be open and prepared to change learning processes based on what the students require and what the assignments require.

OVERCOMING PUSHBACK

When you hear the following types of comments as pushback, be prepared with these positive and honest answers.

I need to be bilingual or multilingual in order to effectively implement translanguaging. Translanguaging is more about students than it is about you, the teacher. It enables them to use all the languages they already know so they can process and absorb new information. You don't need to speak every language; your main responsibility is to support and encourage them. Consider asking students to reach out to their communities through engaging activities that you can conduct in their native languages. If you still feel intimidated because you don't speak your students' native languages, you can gradually implement translanguaging methods by pairing students or carving out time for individual work. For example, have them read in their native language and converse in the target language. They can show their understanding through multilingual presentations.

I do not teach in bilingual or multilingual programs, so translanguaging is irrelevant to my classroom. You can absolutely adopt translanguaging methods in mainstream English-dominant classes and non-multilingual subjects, especially if you are building the capacity to properly cater to CLDs or are building a culturally inclusive and relevant classroom. For example, as a K–12 teacher, you can use bilingual and multilingual texts to model translanguaging, encourage students' speaking and writing in other languages, and make room for authentic multilingual communication. This strengthens your teaching in a diverse nation and exposes students to equitable ways of learning.

New ELL programs cost a lot of money. It's true, and leadership has to resolve this by providing incentives and financial support for you to explore alternative trainings and other opportunities to help you accommodate ELL students. The ELL programs can also be problematic because sometimes the materials are outdated or do not align with the classroom practices you need to implement to accommodate particular students. Be flexible and creative, willing to try new strategies. Each ELL student may require a different approach or materials, which can be intimidating. Explore alternatives and amplify student voice and choice in your approach. Draw from the students' cultures, languages, and communities to find available resources.

THE HACK IN ACTION

Ms. Kellie Brown, an African American teacher from Chicago, has spent over twenty-five years in the Chicago Public Schools system. She has taught language arts (reading, writing, and social studies) to first, third, fourth, fifth, and sixth grades in diverse neighborhoods. In my interview with her, we talked extensively about her experience teaching multilingual learners and reflected on the fact that her classroom makeup has always been predominantly Latinx and African American students. She shared many culturally sustaining and inclusive approaches that have been successful over the years.

Kellie named "labeling" as one of the most effective strategies in her practice. This literally means that she labels objects all around her classroom. She has taught "newcomers" to the US, some of whom only speak one language at home, and of course, that creates language proficiency variations. The labels have been an effective teaching strategy.

Because her students have language variations and diversity, Kellie creatively provides extra support by allowing them to use their home languages while learning English. She uses equivalents and cognates in lessons and activities, total physical language (the use of physical movements, gestures, and other body language to communicate and express feelings, thoughts, and emotions in a way that words cannot), talking and discussions, and literature circles. She also groups students according to their abilities and how well they prepare for activities.

Kellie allows students to write in their home languages, such as Spanish, and do a lot of their work independently. She refrains from translating everything, especially because that is not sustainable, but she also says that she encourages them to be self-sufficient while she provides the necessary support along the way. She uses word isolation in reading activities or when introducing new concepts—helping students break down the text, understand the target vocabulary, make meaning, and connect to the main ideas. She's a huge advocate for graphic organizers, check boxes, small groups, and assistive technology, and she employs conferencing to review content, performance, and student goals.

Thousands of Black, Latinx, and Indigenous students attend schools without same-race or same-ethnicity teachers. Many teachers have limited knowledge about their students' histories and cultures. Bilingual programs promise to nurture students' home languages, but many teachers employ assimilative practices, not equitable ones. All teachers can effectively use translanguaging to help students retain information, and it may help them reconnect with their cultures. Creating and sustaining equitable learning environments requires avoiding the traditional methods that negatively impact students' attitudes about their cultures and languages.

Classroom instruction often underappreciates the depth of students' cultural knowledge and values. As teachers, we can do better in the future than we collectively did in the past. Incorporating translanguaging methods supports every student's learning and gives them opportunities to use their comprehensive linguistic repertoire, boosting their success and confidence in the classroom and beyond.

HACK 4

APPLY EDUCATIONAL TECHNOLOGY

Integrate New Methods That Enhance Equity

*Technology can help our kids become
creators, not just consumers, of information.
It promotes collaboration in ways that get our
kids interested in creating and learning.*
— JOHN D. COUCH, APPLE'S FIRST VICE
PRESIDENT OF EDUCATION

THE PROBLEM: WE RELY ON TECHNOLOGY, YET STRUGGLE TO CATCH UP

THE WORLD OF education has long had problems integrating technology in classrooms. The issues include insufficient teacher training, technological gaps between teachers and students, and the fact that many students are left behind due to inaccessibility. As educators, we can feel like we are constantly struggling to catch up, especially for those teaching the younger generation of students who were exposed to technology at young ages. John D. Couch refers to younger generations as digital natives. Technology wired their brains differently because they have grown up with it. They process information differently, which sometimes translates to not speaking the same language as teachers.

Everyone does their best to navigate technological environments and adopt new tools and technology to maintain meaningful experiences, but educators often need more guidance than they receive. The COVID-19 pandemic further exacerbated preexisting educational inequalities, despite the fact that these issues are relatively new. For example, students in low-resource communities continue to lack access to the internet and necessary technologies. Some educators struggle to adapt to computer-based learning and lack the necessary training. And accessing resources has become more difficult as the number of people requiring assistance has increased globally. And last but equally important, resources have become limited—which impacts our students.

Inaccessible instructional design is harming our students with disabilities. Over seven million students, or 14 percent of all students, identify as having a disability. Eighty-six percent of these students come from backgrounds with diverse cultures or languages (US Department of Education, Office of Special Education Programs, 2019). We see learning disabilities in 34 percent of students in special education. Many students with learning disabilities come from racialized or culturally and linguistically diverse (CLD) backgrounds, and this is a systemic issue. Every racial and ethnic group includes an excess of CLD students. For instance, 27 percent of CLD students are Hispanic and 20 percent are African American, yet only 24.8 percent of students are Hispanic, and 16 percent are African American. It's stunningly obvious that more is going on than the recognition of genuine disabilities.

Considering those numbers, accessibility is a major priority in educational technology, but teachers lack the training to design materials that are accessible, especially for the students that need them. We must take accessibility into account when choosing apps to use in the classroom and carefully consider device capabilities, accessibility features, and instructional materials that appropriately support and enable access to content and educational activities for all learners. In addition, note that accessibility encompasses students with learning or other developmental disabilities, as well as those with sensory or physical disabilities. They all deserve a classroom that serves them and prepares them for success.

Incorporate apps into your teaching to create inclusive, creative, and fun learning experiences.

THE HACK: APPLY EDUCATIONAL TECHNOLOGY

The future of education is rapidly changing, and we must prioritize our preparedness for the future—for ourselves and our students. Technology allows all students to access the curriculum and embrace learning in personalized ways. Many schools use one-on-one technology, putting students who have access to technology in better positions than those without technology. It's essential to be aware of how technology can transform learning and promote inclusive education.

Technology allows teachers to provide accessible content to students with learning disabilities. It can support accessibility through embedded assistance such as text-to-speech, audio, and digital text formats. A plethora of resources exists for you and your students. Allocate time for training, taking risks, and trying new things. Some are free, but others require an investment from leadership or teachers. As you know, most students are already using technology to learn outside the classroom with platforms such as TikTok, YouTube, and Instagram. You can incorporate apps into your teaching to create inclusive, creative, and fun learning experiences.

Educators can work collaboratively to close the technological gaps by gaining the necessary tech knowledge and skills. All education stakeholders need a shared understanding of the ways in which technology may successfully serve the needs of all students.

See Image 4.1 for the Office of Education Technology's recommended guiding principles for early learners.

GUIDING PRINCIPLES IN TECHNOLOGY FOR EARLY LEARNERS

GUIDING PRINCIPLE 1	Accessibility	Develop information, materials, and resources accessible to all learners, regardless of their abilities.
GUIDING PRINCIPLE 2	Engagement	Design learning experiences that are engaging and meaningful to all learners.
GUIDING PRINCIPLE 3	Collaboration	Foster collaboration and communication between learners, their families, and educators.
GUIDING PRINCIPLE 4	Equity	Ensure equitable access to technology and resources for all learners.

Image 4.1: Source: Office of Education Technology.

Students now have access to tools and data all over the world at their fingertips, thanks to advancements in educational technology.

Within the confines of a classroom, learning and instructing may expand without limits. With technological devices, access to the internet, and online collaboration platforms, students can work together with their peers on connected projects regardless of where they are physically located. We are in a position to provide historically under-resourced students with equitable access to high-quality curriculum design and culturally and linguistically relevant content, tailored to meet their accessibility (and other) needs—we can provide them with skills that will prepare them for life beyond the classroom. We must take advantage of the opportunity to construct blended experiences for our students, and take time to think about how we can incorporate technology to shape both pedagogical practices and the learning journeys of our students.

WHAT YOU CAN DO TOMORROW

Consider the criteria established by your school and other relevant resources as you design a strategy to successfully change your classroom into one that is accessible and welcoming of technological advancements. Try a few of these tactics starting tomorrow.

- **Consider your answers to these questions.** Do the approaches I use now encourage individualized learning experiences that are interesting and relevant for the students I teach? In what ways can I integrate my instruction into the real world? In what ways can I utilize technology in the different environments in which I learn? Am I inspiring my pupils to follow their interests and pursue their passions? How do I make sure that all of my students have learning experiences that are accessible and fair for them?

- **Find open educational resources.** If you need extra guidance on how you can accommodate your students, such as building accessible materials for students with disabilities or diversifying mediums of learning, you can find educational resources that are publicly accessible for anyone to access and modify. Individuals or groups create open educational resources (OERs) with minimal, if any, ownership rights. This contrasts with copyrighted and fixed standard curricular materials. OER content is free of charge and may include comprehensive academic programs (some certifications are free too), reinterpretations of already free materials, digital textbooks, curriculum materials for grades K–12, and interactive simulations.

- **Consider language and translation tools.** Employing learning technologies and tools can help bilingual speakers improve their linguistic abilities through features like speech recording, playback, translation, and closed-captioning. They can also enhance language by supporting students' holistic linguistic repertoire (translanguaging strategies). You can alter resources that include translations in both languages. Consider language applications and translation tools (although they are not always as accurate, they can help).

- **Review your students' IEPs/504s.** To create an inclusive classroom, you need to be fully aware of each student's educational situation and needs. Frequently review your students' individualized education plans (IEPs) and Section 504 plans. Familiarize yourself with them as a point of reference for your instructional planning, including your plans for using technology.

- **Incorporate the real world.** Teachers can better inspire their students to learn and grow when they can draw connections between what they're teaching and the world beyond the classroom. Students reap the benefits when teachers integrate current global events into lessons, draw parallels between what they learn inside the classroom and out, and promote awareness of the diverse cultural, social, and political perspectives that students may not have been exposed to otherwise.

- **Create an initial augmented reality (AR) experience.** Students gain a lot from utilizing augmented reality to create scenarios and experiences in which they wouldn't otherwise participate. This also helps eliminate schedule and travel limitations for getting to a particular place. The use of AR technology reduces the amount of time and effort required for setting up gaming experiences, enabling teachers to engage students with the same kind of immersive content that they experience in their daily lives. You may include multiple-choice characters, speech bubbles, open-ended questions, websites, and YouTube videos into their AR experiences. Ask students to capture objects to demonstrate their understanding of the lesson, and provide them with an AR viewer if your school already has one available.

- **Design an accessible and equitable learning environment for all students.** With a little digging, you can find plenty of resources to help you design accessible materials for your students. For example, the International Society for Technology in Education (ISTE) provides the following five teacher standards you can adopt, merge, or modify to cultivate innovative, self-sufficient students.

  1. *Facilitate and inspire student learning and creativity:* Educators continuously improve their practice by learning from and collaborating with others and exploring proven and promising practices that leverage technology to improve student learning.

  2. *Design and develop digital age learning experiences and assessments:* Educators design, develop, and evaluate authentic learning experiences and assessments incorporating contemporary tools and resources to maximize content learning in context and to develop the knowledge, skills, and attitudes identified in the ISTE Standards for Students.

  3. *Model digital age work and learning:* Educators understand local and global societal issues and responsibilities in an evolving

digital culture and exhibit legal and ethical behavior in their professional practices.

4. *Promote and model digital citizenship and responsibility:* Educators understand local and global societal issues and responsibilities in an evolving digital culture and exhibit legal and ethical behavior in their professional practices.

5. *Engage in professional growth and leadership:* Educators take advantage of learning opportunities to grow professionally and model lifelong learning, and they exhibit leadership by demonstrating a vision of technology infusion, participating in shared decision-making and community building, and developing the leadership and technology skills of others.

A BLUEPRINT FOR FULL IMPLEMENTATION

STEP 1: Start small and take risks with technological learning tools.

It's important for students to see that you and the people they look up to attempt new things, make mistakes, and keep trying again. Students must fail in order to learn. Challenges posed by real-world initiatives provide students the chance to try and fail, repeat, and finally succeed. Introduce different ways of learning, such as through music, video, audio, drawing, and other forms of art. Show your students that you are not afraid to try it as well. Start with simple drawings, then advance to sketches. Eventually, some students may create animated drawings, advanced artwork, or videos. Take it one project at a time, see how it goes with your students, and then continue to revise, learn, and expand upon what you have already established. Give yourself some compassion and make the changes you want to see in your classroom.

STEP 2: Personalize learning.

Educators and researchers from all over the world use a wide variety of technologies to provide a more personalized approach to teaching and learning at all grade levels. Our connection with educational technology has evolved as a direct result of the pandemic. While we are looking at different methods to customize education, we must cultivate a culture of human connection and extend grace to our students and ourselves as we process the world around us together. Here are four essential features for personalizing learning: 1) the creation of personalized learning plans; 2) the creation of project challenge-based learning; 3) the tracking of student competency progress; and 4) the multi-year mentoring of students by a teacher.

Incorporating media like movies, audio excerpts, and interactive games is one option you have when considering these best practices. Make use of various technological tools to get immediate feedback on the level of students' understanding, and then use the data to modify your own process. This provides students with more options outside of the standard essay, report, or poster. For instance, you may ask them if they want to show their understanding of a lesson by submitting their work in the form of a multimedia presentation, animated video, augmented reality, or a short film, and let them select whatever option best suits them. Always consider the following three aspects when personalizing lessons: varying activities, amplifying and nurturing student voices, and ensuring all students have equitable access.

STEP 3: Drive student engagement.

To engage your students, begin by identifying available and diverse learning resources and materials in your community and online. If your school uses a set curriculum, you can offer a list of suggestions for at-home and summer reading. Through social media platforms such as LinkedIn, Instagram, Facebook, and Twitter, you may effortlessly communicate with various influential people. Invite these influential people to speak in your class, either in person or through a platform such as Zoom.

Gamified learning features digital games and design tools as a teaching strategy. Students' academic motivation often increases with the anticipation of healthy competition. Gamification can aid in knowledge retention.

Develop guiding questions for the students to answer on their own or in small groups, and either explain or provide a list of academic resources that are pertinent to the topic. Then encourage students to research the material covered in the class using the internet, the library, or the technology provided by your school. For new ideas on engaging students, see the book *Even More Hacking Engagement* by James Sturtevant.

STEP 4: Tap into students' expertise and experience.

Teachers who feel a lack of technological confidence compared to students may be reluctant to use technology in the classroom. Encourage your students to use their technological abilities to everyone's advantage and create an inclusive, accessible tech environment by allowing them to have autonomy in the learning process. Your students are digital natives. They have spent their whole lives working with computers and the internet. Feel free to ask for help with technology or to collaborate on class activities and projects. Give students a chance to think imaginatively about how to tackle the assignments. Ask them questions that will help them to apply the concepts, ideas, and principles they have learned to real-world situations. Open-ended problems and challenge-based projects will spur them to evaluate several perspectives that lead to various responses and are even more powerful when they can present their thought processes in a medium of their choice.

STEP 5: Incorporate challenge- or problem-based learning.

Problem-based learning requires students to come up with a solution to a clearly defined real-world problem. Technology is a great tool for cultivating collaboration among students and also helps them work with each other by sharing ideas and relying on each other's strengths and skillsets. Some students may be more advanced than others, which gives you the opportunity to facilitate their learning and offer more autonomy. By using this method, you encourage your students to reflect, develop critical thinking skills, and experiment with new ways to demonstrate their understanding. Your main goal is to have students learn something new.

You can design a problem-based activity around topics such as climate change, immigration laws, social justice movements, and the water crises in different parts of the US.

Consider these steps to design a problem-based K–12 project on climate issues.

- Begin by researching the current impact of climate change on the K–12 student population. Consider local, regional, and global effects, as well as potential physical, mental, and economic health impacts.

- Develop a learning goal by identifying the specific knowledge, skills, and attitudes that students should gain from the project.

- Create an engaging title that captures the essence of the project and motivates students to want to learn about climate change.

- Determine the grade level and type of project that best aligns with the learning goal.

- Select appropriate materials and resources that can support the project, such as books, videos, articles, simulations, and hands-on activities.

- Develop activities that actively engage students in the project and ensure that the work is meaningful and enjoyable.

- Design assessments that measure student learning and provide feedback to the instructor.

- Establish a timeline for the project, including a plan for evaluation and review.

- Make sure to provide an opportunity for students to share their projects with peers and the larger community.

STEP 6: Consider project-based learning.

In project-based learning, you can expect students to create a product to show that they understand the material. The work is often based on real-world problems and includes information from various subjects. If you set up lessons and support them correctly, students can learn in-demand skills like creativity, leadership, and collaboration. It also gets them involved in complex world problems that help them meet critical thinking standards. Lastly, with this approach, you are mainly looking to evaluate the final product that students produce.

Divide students up into groups and ask them to identify a problem they can solve with the available technology and tools. Give them guidelines and a timeline, and request that they establish a means of communication so they can stay in contact as they work on the project. Once they have everything they need, they are free to delegate responsibilities to each team member and to choose how they will present the problem and recommend a solution as a team. Encourage them to choose from a podcast, video, website, photobook, poem, blog, article, or artwork. Regardless of constraints, you can typically implement this to support any mandated curriculum.

STEP 7: Streamline differentiated learning.

Incorporating edtech and adaptive tools is another way to discover unique teaching methods. You don't need to reinvent the wheel when there is already enough technology available that is tailored to specific student needs. Using a flexible approach to time-based tasks, for example, allows students who finish their work more quickly to move on to extension tasks while allowing students who finish their work at a more leisurely pace to finish their exercise.

Many platforms allow you to create graphic organizers that align with your lesson plans. Research free templates and tools that can generate interactive graphic organizers. Encourage students to use educational technology to achieve their learning goals.

Try a pre-assessment using Google Forms, student response games like Kahoot! or Quizizz, and other platforms that are functionally equivalent. These tools often motivate students and engage them in the learning because they can participate confidentially when interacting with other students. Even though other students cannot see their direct responses, you can still gather data behind the scenes and use it to adjust the lesson accordingly.

Allow time for one-on-ones with each student. When students are working on their own, you can talk with them individually, encourage their ideas, and provide support with complex topics.

Check on their comfort level with particular devices, features, or platforms to ensure they are comfortable using the technology while working on projects. You can also use technology such as Google Classroom or your school's selected Learning Management System to incorporate flexible grouping and to assign lessons to specific students, as opposed to the whole class. You can meet with students asynchronously or use Zoom to create virtual breakout rooms with small groups.

STEP 8: Utilize social media.

Many risks accompany unsupervised access to social media, but there are also numerous advantages to using technology for education. Our approach can be a healthy balance, including abiding by school standards and ensuring parental consent before adopting social media in the classroom. After deciding on a platform or asking your students and their parents what they are most comfortable with, clearly explain the goals, intentions, and purposes of using the particular platform. (For example, sharing curriculum content, strengthening relationships and communication with parents, developing digital citizenship, and staying connected in hybrid learning environments.)

You and your students can then work together to create an official class social media account, which you can use to teach digital literacy skills, provide opportunities to practice digital citizenship in a supervised setting, and eliminate the popular misconception that social media is only for fun and games. When you develop an account together as a classroom, your students will feel a sense of unity and may even feel comfortable engaging on the social media account by asking questions, helping their peers, and collaborating. Set ground rules together and make sure to infuse brave space components so you can continue to foster an inclusive, accessible environment for all students.

STEP 9: Use mobile technology for communication, collaboration, and secure information storage.

As you know, phones and other mobile devices were once commonly considered taboo in the classroom. Now, students are more likely to engage when they use their mobile devices for learning purposes. Mobile devices make it feasible to immerse students in realistic settings, allowing them to engage in interactive simulations. Educators can shift their paradigm from an optional use of mobile devices in the classroom to a required use. If you don't already, start seeing mobile technologies as integral to the teaching and learning process. Students already use technology in their daily routines (some more than others, depending on access). Teach them to study more effectively with mobile learning and encourage them to learn outside of the classroom and at their own pace. With mobile devices, students can readily access information, communicate with you and their classmates, and keep track of learning timelines (such as due dates, reminders, and exams).

STEP 10: Incorporate creative applications and platforms.

Interactive tools, applications, and platforms inspire student creativity. They also help students to explore a subject or problem from different viewpoints. Also, diversifying learning methods benefits your students because some prefer working with nontraditional materials and media, while others prefer digital tools. Give your students the gift of confidence to amplify their digital capabilities, exposing them to a level of diversity to employ various learning resources, platforms, and technologies to accomplish the same goal.

Suggest specific creative applications and platforms, especially those that students are already familiar with. Discipline- or course-specific mobile apps are effective not just for delivering content but also for achieving learning goals.

STEP 11: Create accessible instructional materials.

Students with disabilities are more likely to participate and have more autonomy or independence in classrooms that are designed with them in mind, and this arrangement benefits all students. Revise your course material designs to make sure they are accessible to all students. This is part of global consumption: encouraging teachers to design materials that meet all student needs and instructional design requirements and expectations. It is also a requirement by law in most states.

Format every document properly. Add accessibility tags in every PDF for those with special needs, and use the built-in default heading styles in your word processing program. Use the built-in list feature to help you properly build bulleted lists that help students using screen-reader software to know how many items are included.

All images must be accompanied by descriptive text unless you explicitly mark them as decorative. Avoid illustrative textual elements. Include closed-captions for all videos used in your lessons or activities. Ensure the contrast between the colors you're using is strong and easy to read. Incorporate descriptive links with brief descriptions of what the student will see when they click them. You can find an activity that helps teach advocacy for students with disabilities in Appendix C.1.

(Note: Do not include blinking, strobing, or gliding movements or images, as they can disrupt students and interfere with their learning and can also cause seizures in some students.)

STEP 12: Encourage storyboarding to simplify concepts and enhance knowledge retention.

Give students the freedom to create personalized learning road maps or storyboard concepts. This aids in organizing and presenting course materials in a way that keeps the student interested, such as through storytelling, interactive lessons, or other forms of engagement. Give your students control over the visual style and interactivity of the presentation by choosing from a wide variety of animations and interactions, such as photos, sounds, icons, charts, and infographics that help them make meaning and achieve the learning objectives.

They can start by drawing and storyboarding at the beginning of each lesson as part of their routine. Then encourage them to share their process with other students to gauge if there are other interpretations of the same idea. You can promote innovative and creative learning through idea sharing. Related formative assessment strategies include the creation of storyboards, picture stories, gallery collections, concept maps and infographics, and audio recordings of processes.

If students are having a hard time coming up with storyboards or are hesitant to give it a try—you can share a model you create as an example. Consider employing a word storyboard (also known as a text-based storyboard) using apps like Pages, Word, Google Docs, PowerPoint or Keynote. I have also used Keynote to organize my storyboards and then shared them as pictures for my students or colleagues to use as examples. Only include storyboards if your approach is strategic and you know why, how, and when you and your students can utilize this tool.

Always keep your learning objectives in mind. Make sure your entire storyboard content connects to an objective. Keep it all equitable and accessible by providing the proper tools with features, devices, and platforms for all students. To simplify the process, choose a storyboard template that is appropriate for you and your students, but allow them to propose other choices. Students who need an extra push will appreciate having more options.

For multilingual students, encourage them to be creative and include texts in their home language. Remember the basics—a good storyboard should have the following: a subject, concept, or process. It should include text, images, or icons to accompany word storyboards, and if converted to video, it should have a voiceover or narration. Make it interactive or engaging. However, it does not have to be perfect to be effective—and there's no such thing anyway. See an example of an app creation project using storyboarding in Appendix C.2.

OVERCOMING PUSHBACK

You may hear technology-related pushback from colleagues and parents. Here's how I respond to these common concerns.

Privacy issues concern me. Take this valid fear seriously. Still, there are so many benefits to using technology for learning purposes, and regulations are in place to assist with privacy issues. The Family Educational Rights and Privacy Act (FERPA) and the Children's Online Privacy Protection Act (COPPA) address data regulations for children under age thirteen and help protect students' privacy online in school settings. However, you, your administrators, and your students' parents or guardians should evaluate app privacy policies before using them in the classroom. We can use technology for good or for bad, so let's use it to create a community of digital citizens and to amplify intellect. Finally, double-check your school's regulations around technology in the classroom. Schools are usually able to build safe and secure internet environments for students, ensuring access to age-appropriate information without danger and confirming that student information is secure and not shared or used illegally.

It is impossible to keep up with the latest technologies, so I'd rather use methods that have been working for me. Fear is normal when it comes to trying new tools and approaches in the classroom. You are training students who will face new challenges inside and outside of the classroom, and it is okay to learn together. Give yourself grace and remain open to learning from your students too. Many tech-savvy students will excitedly share new tips and tricks. And others can gain the courage to try new things when they see you try. In addition, identify your school or district's tech support and resources, as well as professional development opportunities. You do not need to know everything; all you need is an open mind and a willingness to experiment. Also, you do not have to change the way you teach to incorporate new tools that interest your students. Consider facilitating their education without becoming an expert on a specific device, tool, or feature.

Using technology is a distraction that disrupts the classroom culture and keeps students from focusing on their work. Students become distracted whether or not they have technology in the classroom. Technology, however, can be a wonderfully effective tool to keep students engaged in ways that lock them in the moment. Try different tools and apps to see which ones are most effective for your students, and encourage them to be creative and create unique solutions as they engage with different tools.

It is overwhelming to manage technical difficulties that prohibit students from collaborating or completing digital projects. One of the worst nightmares is dealing with technical issues that stall the education process. Consider having students share a copy of their work in collaboration mode so you always have access to it; this can minimize issues and save time on troubleshooting. Provide students with a brief orientation to collaborative work using cloud-sharing platforms, and show them how to use auto-save. That way, if something happens to a student's device, you (and the rest of the classmates, depending on settings) can access a copy. Additionally, before students begin projects or activities, ensure that their devices and the applications they are using are up to date. If all this fails, remember that we can only control what we can; give yourself and your students grace. Technology is not perfect.

THE HACK IN ACTION

I had the privilege of teaching and incorporating alternative curricula through collaboration with a four-year university diversity office, local high schools, and the Federal TRIO Programs. The goal was to expand students' perspectives on creativity and spark interest in the rapidly growing fields in our society. TRIO is an outreach and student assistance initiative by the federal government that seeks to assist students from under-resourced communities, such as first-generation college students and those with disabilities, to develop academically from middle school to post-secondary education. I instructed a Creative Technology course in the summer of 2020, and most of my students were CLDs.

I had thirty-six students in grades ten, eleven, and twelve. They all had access to devices, specifically iPads, which came pre-loaded with the applications I planned to teach about through the program. I applied different approaches to challenge students but also inspire and spark their interests over time. I used the Everyone Can Create curriculum by Apple Education, which was a huge time-saver over having to create lesson plans and project templates from scratch. It also included in-depth rubrics and more resources for all subjects. I spent the first week teaching them about creative writing, then I transitioned to drawing, videos, and audio.

I asked them to write about someone or something that meant a lot to them and submit it with a piece of art they created or appreciated. I encouraged and supported them to express themselves through photos, music, art, writing, and other forms of creativity that helped to bring their world into the classroom. They could use their mobile devices, graphic design platforms, and interactive applications to create art that showed their newly acquired skills. The goal of this activity was to encourage students to try new things and also inspire their peers who are more reluctant to take risks. Here are examples from four students and what they shared in class (shared here with their permission).

Jamila shared the following note after showing pictures of people and items:

> *"The images I shared mean a lot to me. My friend Da'Vontae Brown was born on May 5, 2004, and passed away May 1, 2020. We were very good friends, but his passing definitely changed me and the people around me. So that's why he's hanging up on my wall because we won't ever forget about him. Then I recently made a collage of pictures of the people I love and care about. I'll soon be adding more pictures of people I'm recently getting pictures with. So my wall will be filled up with people who make me genuinely happy and make me feel loved and cared for."*

Aria created the four pieces of artwork shown in Images 4.2 through 4.5, and she shared how much they meant to her. She enjoyed drawing and putting her talents to work, and her creations inspired other students to try new features and applications on their iPads.

Image 4.2

Image 4.3

Image 4.4

Image 4.5

Aneia shared a song with the class, "Myself" by Layton Greene, and described how it helped her during a challenging time in her life. She also described a lesson she learned in the process. Here are the words she shared with the class:

> *"I chose this song because I love it and because I feel like I was in that position before. I was in a toxic relationship and felt like I wasn't good enough for him and that I wasn't making him happy or being his peace. I also chose this song because I feel like when you're listening to it, it uplifts you. It makes you have more love for yourself! and makes you want to know your worth. This song means a lot! I think this song is mostly about not knowing your worth and being taken for granted. The song is also about loving the person and having feelings but not getting the same energy and affection back. The song is sad because it's like she really expresses her feelings and what she went through in the song. That's why the song is good because it's important for girls who want to date or are dating. They need to know that if he's not making you happy or uplifting you, then it's not a healthy relationship. Y'all have to put in the same energy for both to be happy!"*

This is the kind of learning experience that truly makes school more personal and organic.

Twinkle shared the following description of a challenge they had been dealing with before finding an outlet, and they even went an extra step to learn a new skill. (I was so proud of them, especially because they incorporated lines, shapes, and colors as we had discussed in our first unit on creativity.) This was an extra-credit activity I offered students to do—to experiment and try a new skill that they could share with the class. See Twinkle's work in Image 4.6.

> *"Lately, I've been a little stressed because of the amount of work I've had. On my iPad, I have this app called Procreate, and I never really understood how to use its features. So I watched a YouTube video on some drawings to draw on there, and this lady showed us how to make mandalas. I found them therapeutic, and I started to draw them. They are not perfect, but I just started them. On Instagram, I used to watch people draw something and then merge colors to create a really cool effect, and I finally learned how to do it!"*

Image 4.6

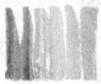

The role of the teacher has expanded beyond the confines of the traditional classroom to incorporate remote learning. There has been no shift in instruction; rather, technology has replaced more conventional methods. Teachers can now provide accessible materials to all students, including those with accessibility needs, allowing the teachers the ability to teach in the same way but with better materials. The Office of Educational Technology provides instructors with strategies on how to utilize technology in the classroom, with a focus on building good relationships with parents and early educators. In addition, states and schools also have standards that can guide educators in technology integration. With the right training and resources, you can successfully transform your classroom into a tech-friendly space and provide students with opportunities to learn, create, explore, innovate, think critically, and solve real-world problems.

ADAPT ASSESSMENTS

Shift Away from Standard Assessment Dependency

Culturally inclusive assessment is essential to providing equitable and meaningful instruction in K-12 education. It ensures that all students' diverse experiences, backgrounds, and perspectives are reflected in the curriculum, instruction, and assessment and provide an opportunity for students to learn in an environment that is both culturally relevant and responsive.
— Tracey Tokuhama-Espinosa

THE PROBLEM: CURRENT ASSESSMENT PRACTICES ARE RARELY CULTURALLY INCLUSIVE, RESPONSIVE, AND RELEVANT

RESEARCH FROM THE National Education Association indicates that Black, Latinx, and Indigenous students, as well as certain Asian students, encounter racial bias on standardized assessments from early education through college. Assessment has remained mostly constant, and little emphasis has been placed on providing students with fair and equitable ways to measure and show their learning.

Standardized testing, whether on a mass or micro level, highlights the distinction between testing all students in the same manner to meet a particular end goal and testing to ensure that all assessments are suitable and inclusive of all students. The latter is not always the case, as federal K–12 education legislation mandates states to verify that students are achieving assessment standards. As a result, teachers have little to no flexibility to adapt their assessment strategies or their curriculum to meet all student needs.

Furthermore, states rely on this data to evaluate schools and publicly report on them. As a direct consequence, educators are under continual pressure to evaluate the progress of their classes, so many are "teaching to the test." When it comes to diversity and inclusion, current practices are far behind regarding designing culturally inclusive, responsive, and relevant assessments. This continues to harm students who come from various cultural and linguistic backgrounds.

Historically, the predominant mode of teaching English to bilingual children has been English immersion, sometimes known as a sink-or-swim approach, and pieces of this practice are still in use today. From the 1920s to the 1960s, there were few, if any, viable programs for remediation. In order for students to grow in their overall understanding, schools forced them to remain in the same grade until they achieved a certain level of English competence. Additionally, before the implementation of the Every Child Succeeds Act (implemented in 2015, replacing the previous version, the No Child Left Behind Act created in 2002), the federal government didn't mandate linguistic requirements.

Fast forward to the present day: the current standards and regulations, which depend on the classification of language learners, exacerbate inequalities by isolating multilingual students and maintaining assimilative practices that restrict linguistic diversity and freedom. Similarly, there is a substantial emphasis on state standards, federal and state laws, and procedures to integrate multiple cultures and languages in mainstream classrooms; this scenario continues to be a struggle for educators and students. Fewer states continue to implement Common Core consortia tests, while others are leaning toward building their own distinctive assessment systems that comprise a combination of Common Core and tailored components. For that reason, the need for equitable assessments is particularly pressing, as we have to do right by culturally and linguistically diverse students, who are frequently affected the most.

THE HACK: ADAPT ASSESSMENTS

According to the National Education Association, we must create assessments that represent the comprehensive spectrum of student learning and abilities, including creativity, critical thinking, and teamwork, in addition to students' prior knowledge and linguistic and cultural backgrounds. This work will lead to more effective assessment methods that properly serve all students' intellectual, social, and emotional needs and disrupt a long history of racially biased assessment policies and practices.

> *It is about time that we collaboratively push for equitable assessments.*

The field of education has an urgent need for assessments that inform teachers about students' intellectual, social, and emotional development in real time. Unfortunately, most classroom assessments don't take into account each student's uniqueness and complexity. For teachers who put students first, we value each student as an individual. We believe that each student brings value and individuality because of the way they think, how they look, where they come from, how they feel, and what language they speak. Many of our students' best qualities hide in plain sight until we use assessments to box them in.

Comparing monolingual students' performance in both content and language to multilingual students' assessment results yields inaccurate and unfair interpretations. It completely disregards the complexities of multilingual experiences. Because content knowledge assessments judge how well students use the dominant "academic language," it makes sense instead to use translanguaging (TL) assessments that respect students' different ways of using language and authentic methods for expressing and demonstrating their knowledge. In the process of rethinking and reconstructing assessments, we can ask ourselves: How can we make assessments more inclusive, diverse, and sensitive to the experiences that students have had in their lives?

In order for us to adapt assessments to benefit students and achieve our desired outcomes, we must shift to focus on the student populations in the classroom by: 1) using appropriate language that is accessible to all students when designing assessment objectives and outcomes, 2) acknowledging the differences among students during the planning stages of an assessment, 3) developing or using assessment tools that are appropriate for multicultural students, and 4) being intentional about using assessment results to enhance learning for all students. Making this a reality is more than just being attentive to students' cultural and linguistic needs. It also requires students to be active participants throughout the whole assessment process, according to the National Institute for Learning Outcomes Assessment.

WHAT YOU CAN DO TOMORROW

The goal is for teachers to create culturally sensitive assessments that promote all students' holistic learning. It is about time that we collaboratively push for equitable assessments, joining efforts with teachers who are already making tangible changes in their classrooms but often face pushback. Assessment issues will continue to persist if we continue to ignore discrepancies. We will inadequately assess students' academic performance, and our recommendations based on their reported performances may not be relevant to improving their academic outcomes beyond primary education. The performance disparity implies that learners who are competent in informal and daily contexts may struggle in more structured environments, necessitating alternative strategies to demonstrate their knowledge. Here are a handful of strategies for you to consider:

- **Run a diagnostic test.** To make sure each student is getting the most out of their education, a diagnostic test may help you identify their unique strengths and areas for improvement. This may also help you figure out the best method to teach new content to all of your students, assess which ones are having trouble and need more attention, and learn more about how your CLDs are processing the information. Consider these diagnostic tests:

▸ **Cognitive Diagnostic Assessment (CDA)** - This test identifies students' strengths, weaknesses, and levels of proficiency in specific skills, and the results can help inform instruction and assessment design.

▸ **Diagnostic Classification Model (DCM)** - This diagnostic test helps teachers identify which items on an assessment are most suitable for different types of learners, and it can help teachers tailor their instruction to meet the needs of all students.

▸ **Criterion-Referenced Tests** - This diagnostic test helps teachers identify what students know and can do, and it can help inform instruction and assessment design.

• **Research appropriate language that is accessible to all students.** Whether in an English language class or a "mainstream" class, chances are you will encounter multilingual students who will benefit from using their holistic linguistic repertoire to comprehend information. You can find creative ways to provide language support or normalize multilingualism in your classroom. Keep in mind that you may have students who are unfamiliar with a particular subject matter or cultural references in the material or assessments. Assessments created with a range of learners in mind better reflect student growth.

- **Consider assessment tools that are appropriate and accommodate students' needs.** Your students have preferred learning styles, whether visual, auditory, kinesthetic, or a mixture of all options. Visual learners prefer to observe and are more likely to succeed after seeing you or someone else demonstrate what is required of them, or they may also prefer the use of images, graphics, and charts to grasp new concepts. They are more likely to follow a clear and direct path, such as written lists, instructions, and guidelines.

  Auditory learners prefer learning information by hearing, and they are more likely to retain information or effectively follow instructions after hearing them from you. They are comfortable with receiving verbal instructions via mobile devices, prefer watching or listening to videos, and may even choose audiobooks over reading physical books. Additionally, they may appreciate using sounds or noises in projects and other activities.

  Lastly, experience is the best teacher for kinesthetic or tactile learners. They prefer hands-on experiences to better understand and retain information. It is important to identify your students' preferences so you can incorporate them while assessing students throughout the school year.

- **Employ co-creating methods.** Students are stakeholders, and the co-creating process is student-centered. This means students can and should be active participants at various levels, including the construction of learning outcome statements, the selection and development of assessment tools, and the collection and analysis of data and its interpretation. Employing co-creative techniques with students enhances the impact, engagement, motivation, and metacognitive reflection of evaluations, resulting in enhanced learning.

In other words, when assessments are conducted with students, they are more productive and efficient. Through a critical lens and in accordance with feminist, social, and community engagement pedagogies, the principles of co-creation enable us to examine and eradicate inequities between knowledge producers (both teachers and students). To affirm student experiences, improve data quality, and create a multidimensional understanding of trustworthy evidence, you must treat students as experts in their own lived experiences and include them as key partners in the process. This validates and addresses the identities and cultural backgrounds of racialized students.

- **Use nontraditional methods, such as digital storybooks, to evaluate your students.** Digital storybooks are engaging and personal, providing an organic picture of students' learning and the application of that information in a natural context they can share with others. It motivates students to reflect on their educational experiences and construct a narrative that describes their academic development, including ways in which they plan to put what they have learned into practice.

- **Investigate related formative and summative assessments.** Reveal which of your existing teaching strategies are not producing the desired results, allowing you to better tailor your lessons to the needs of your students. The purpose of formative assessment is twofold: first, to monitor student development; second, to hone classroom practices. You must know how various student populations learn so you can tailor your assessments. For summative assessments, some students may be anxious or intimidated to take part in traditional quizzes and assessments because they lack confidence in their skills. Others may have trouble understanding STEAM topics or reading fluently. Summative assessments enable you to identify the gaps and build specialized interventions to fill them in.

A BLUEPRINT FOR FULL IMPLEMENTATION

STEP 1: Determine what you want to assess.

Narrow down the precise information or set of abilities you will assess before administering tests. Then you can see how each student is progressing and tailor your approach to ensure they get the knowledge and abilities they need.

STEP 2: Create relevant and meaningful assessment content.

Use different examples and points of view to help people of different ages, abilities, genders, ethnicities, races, socioeconomic statuses, and interests understand specific ideas. It makes a significant difference when students feel connected to the materials. The key is to evaluate our students and use what we learn to inform, empower, and motivate them in useful, meaningful ways. Keep creativity, collaboration, communication, and critical thinking in mind as you develop equitable assessments and transform how you measure student understanding and how they demonstrate their knowledge.

Lastly, ask students for feedback as a means to ensure meaningful assessment. Create a questionnaire to distribute after each significant lesson or exam, and then discuss the findings with students and make necessary modifications for the future. I have had times when an exam appeared to be extremely difficult for students based on their performance, and I assumed they did not understand the material—but when I asked students where I could have gone wrong, I learned that several factors were at play: not having enough time between several assessments, transitioning from paper to digital formats, or simply not reviewing the information or vocabulary enough times (this varies by student). We decided to create mini-assessments together, schedule more review sessions, and learn vocabulary through games, group activities, and silent reflection time in the future. When we adjusted the pace and focused on understanding the content rather than on preparing for another one of many assessments, the students performed much better.

Pay attention to how your students interpret questions, activities, and assignments differently, and collect and review their feedback about the learning. Take note of the linguistic diversity in your classroom, and encourage students to express themselves in different ways to demonstrate their understanding of classroom activities. Allow students to ask questions and use simpler language to clarify or explain complex texts.

STEP 3: Select assessment strategies that maximize performance for various learners.

Identify key facts to help students concentrate on the subject you are teaching, and encourage them to act out new vocabulary words or complex concepts. For students who speak other languages, invite them to create a skit with the new terminology and use translation materials or technology with closed-captions on video activities. Offer additional support or tools, whether graphic charts, graphs, checklists, or infographics, that are pertinent to the activity at hand. Create varied exercises to offer your students choices on how to effectively demonstrate their understanding and expertise.

STEP 4: Ensure that your assessments are in line with your learning goals.

When deconstructing your standards to develop assessments, link your assessments to learning outcomes, and teach accordingly. Consider the following questions: How can you make this process more inclusive and equitable? How will your students complete the tasks? What activities will they do, and how are they relevant to the objectives and standards? What's the timeframe? What resources, support, or accessibility accommodations will they need?

Use the backward instructional design method. Grant Wiggins and Jay McTighe introduced this method in their book *Understanding By Design*. It allows you to plan instruction by beginning with the desired outcome and working backward to implement your plan in three phases. Using their concept as a starting place, the following are my versions of the three phases and the associated questions.

> **Phase 1: Determine desired outcomes** by taking into account the course, unit, and lesson objectives. As you gradually narrow down on the most useful information, ask yourself these four questions:
> - ► What should my students see, read, hear, and research?
> - ► What else should I expose them to?
> - ► What knowledge and abilities should they acquire?

► What are the key concepts and ideas that students should retain?

Phase 2: Choose acceptable key measures of success for students to demonstrate understanding, knowledge, and growth, such as tests and performance assignments. This phase will provide a deeper understanding of what proof students might offer to demonstrate they have attained or are making progress toward achieving the predetermined learning objectives. This phase focuses on two questions:

► How will I know if my students achieved the outcomes they were hoping for?

► What will I accept as proof of a student's proficiency and understanding?

Phase 3: Plan instruction and learning activities. After you have established goals and evaluation techniques, you have a great foundation for building teaching methods that will be the most effective in equipping students with the tools and knowledge they need to achieve the objective. Ask yourself these questions:

► What enabling information and capabilities will my students need in order to successfully perform and achieve the outcomes they seek?

► What exercises will provide my students with the necessary information and skills?

► Considering performance objectives, what will I need in order to teach, coach, facilitate, and demonstrate, and how should I do it?

► What resources, materials, and tools will help us achieve these objectives?

STEP 5: Clearly define your assessment expectations to your students long before the assessment.

Students have a greater chance of succeeding when they are aware of what teachers expect from them. Although this is an advantage for all students, it is particularly helpful to students who come from culturally and linguistically diverse backgrounds.

Establish your goals and general expectations on your syllabus, ensuring that you prepare for every area of the class. Review it with the class, and make sure they get an idea of what the class will entail. You could also build in a syllabus activity to check their understanding before moving forward with new learning material. For multilingual students, you can provide a translated syllabus in their home language and encourage them to share a copy with their parents or guardians. Emphasize the main takeaways of the lessons or the activities, and give students collaborative time in class to discuss and ask questions about their assignment or the rubric. (Offer rubrics with detailed expectations and a reward scale.)

STEP 6: Develop a clear but flexible assessment plan.

Define your assessment methods and objectives. When you share clear formats, guidelines, and expectations, you are helping students to prepare efficiently and to show dependable, substantial proof of their learning. Integrate periodic assessments in other curriculum components like skill-development exercises, class discussions, group projects, and individual assignments. To ensure student understanding and readiness, communicate about the assessment in various ways, including assignment summaries in the syllabus and rubrics with objectives and assessment criteria. Track student learning by giving the assessment at the appropriate moment (not too early or too late). Instead of consistently comparing students to their classmates, who are at various levels and also have varied language and cultural diversity, analyze the data and compare students to their own progress and development. Share assessment results with the students within a suitable amount of time, highlighting areas for strength and development. Allow yourself ample time to determine whether the assessment was accurate and dependable, and if not, tell the students about it and equitably change comments and marks. Together with your students, reflect and revise to ensure future advancements and necessary modifications to your assessments.

STEP 7: Design adaptable assessments.

This approach could be one way to create assessment equity and level the playing field for culturally and linguistically diverse students. Make different assessments for the same abilities and comprehension and target the same learning objectives. You may provide extra scaffolding, such as outlines, examples, summaries, or quotes to help students think through their arguments and practice critical thinking and problem-solving skills.

Provide students with choices for streamlined, condensed, or shorter make-up exams. They could submit their exam answers in a different format that still showcases their understanding of the material. Integrate technology into your assessments and allow students who must complete an assessment but lack access to it in a particular place or at a particular time to do so. This is important, especially now that technology plays an ever-larger role in student success. You can learn more about using technology for equity in Hack 4.

Give students reasonable time frames for making up or redoing assessments (remember SMART goals from Chapter 1). This allows students to showcase their understanding at their pace without feeling the pressure of time constraints. Create project-based assessments with a range of options and components so students can show their learning in the most applicable and reasonable ways that account for their linguistic and cultural practices. These could be both individual and collaborative projects that still measure the same outcomes.

STEP 8: Confirm that students understand your assessment platform.

As a starting point, take mock assessments on the chosen platform before the actual one, and ensure that students are ready or have their questions answered. We can't assume that students who are new to our classes automatically know how to use particular devices or platforms. Gauge student familiarity with components like hyperlinks, embedded films or audio, and mouse navigation. Make sure they are comfortable with the methods for going from one question to the next, skipping parts and then returning to them, saving answers (if that's an option or feature), and submitting final answers. It may not always be obvious or simple because all students have different exposures to different platforms.

STEP 9: Reimagine the role of assessment.

Ponder your answers to these questions as you reimagine the role of assessment to help your students achieve their learning objectives.

- Have you collected proof of student learning and validated diverse ways of gaining and showing information using various methods?

- In what ways does enabling students to communicate in their home language effectively implement student agency?

- How do you approach intersectionality (such as race, ethnicity, class, gender identity, age, and class)?

- How much do demographic indicators serve as cultural proxies?

OVERCOMING PUSHBACK

Here's how you might address common questions and concerns about assessments. Pushback around this topic may be more about the fear of change or resistance to a potentially time-consuming new process. But the benefits of adapting our assessments are so instrumental to our students' success that you'll want to be ready with good explanations.

I prefer traditional testing because I care about academic honesty. Most assessment policies and procedures support the notions that students will not cheat on traditional tests and that traditional tests do not demonstrate how well students can apply their knowledge, skills, and attitudes in the real world. Traditional testing often puts CLDs and ELL students at a disadvantage. Fortunately, there are creative ways to incorporate technology-based exams into your classroom without jeopardizing academic integrity. During testing, you can use classroom applications that give you control over student devices. You can also include collaborative assessments in which students can work together on specific parts of the exam to eliminate cheating.

Including other languages and cultures in my assessments will be incredibly difficult and may be detrimental to students who are already at a disadvantage. First, ask yourself where this assumption is coming from. Is it because you believe students need more English to help them understand the evaluated information? What is the alternative? Have you tried it and discovered that "disadvantaged" students are negatively impacted? Significant evidence exists that including other languages can boost students' performance and understanding. Consider other cultural signifiers that you can include. For example, when talking about "soccer" in class with immigrant students, you could change their terminology to "football." Sometimes those small adjustments make a significant difference in how students internalize information.

**It is time-consuming to develop assessments that accommo-
date CLDs, as I am a monolingual teacher.** This is a common
concern among educators, especially given the lack of training in
teacher education programs. It will take time to implement culturally relevant assessment strategies. First you must understand
students' cultural modes of communication and participation in
order to create culturally appropriate means for them to demonstrate their knowledge. Acknowledge that multilingual students
use their own language(s) to facilitate learning and comprehension
of the instruction. These are critical steps toward changing your
methods. Consider collaborating with a diverse group of educators and informing leadership about this critical need. It takes a
team effort to develop a sustainable approach that will benefit students and teachers in the long run.

**Assessments are culturally neutral and do not represent
just one particular culture.** This is not the case. Education policies and practices traditionally represent White mainstream
English and are Eurocentric. For example, traditional curricula
focus on the contributions of White European individuals and
nations, often leaving out the perspectives of racialized communities, and schools often teach only English and use it as the primary medium of instruction. This can be exclusionary to students
who don't speak English as their first language. The assessments
that some believe are unbiased actually predominantly represent
White culture. They have contributed to decades of inaccurate
evaluation of CLDs and caused many frustrations in diverse communities. Racialized students do not feel connected to the materials that are the basis of instruction and assessment. Determine
where allowing members of racialized groups to offer input and
feedback might improve diversity and amplify their contribution
in the process of shifting your assessment.

THE HACK IN ACTION

As a former student who struggled mightily with tests and quizzes, one aspect of teaching that I focused on extensively was assessment. To make sure my students wouldn't be overwhelmed by tests, I always familiarized myself with new tools, features, or gadgets before putting them to use in class, and then made sure students were familiar with them too. I accommodated students in ways that benefited them and put them at ease, whether that meant giving extra time on an exam, changing the format, or offering translated questions. All the methods I used for assessing my class could work for young adult learners and maybe some younger students.

I posted a blog post weekly to reflect the materials that we had created each week—these were individual entries, similar to journal writings. I would read them at the end of each week and then provide constructive feedback to my students. For example, the first unit was about learning the difference between schooling and education. Students were to make a distinction between the two based on readings and videos we watched together as a class. I would then post a question to the classroom forum and ask them to create a response and submit it using excerpts from the movie and readings.

In relation to social justice, I would pose such questions: In what ways does social justice play a role in the classroom? Should schools be the place to discuss social issues? And if so, why? If not there, where else in society might we try to solve issues of social justice? Simply change the language if your school restricts the use: ask students which individual is at an advantage and who is not in any given scenario.

I provided simple directions, requiring students to take the time to read and answer the comments of at least one peer's post. I instructed them to either dispute a point they made or expand their thought further, then ask one question to encourage additional discussion. There was no strict word limit requirement; however, when replying to another participant, students were required to compose at least four to five complete sentences. They also had to give careful consideration to how they intended to communicate their response and encourage brave spaces to draw people in and foster dialogue rather than call individuals out. This allowed me to conduct ongoing assessments, as well as witness their skill development and ability to apply the brave space rules we had created together as a class.

As the school year progressed, I expanded on what we had covered and further encouraged students to consider the relationship between social justice and their schooling or education by focusing on the significance of identity and the unique challenges that various student subgroups face. Eventually, I started to assign them to write blogs bi-weekly, based on students' feedback and the pace of the content we were learning. I incorporated both digital and paper format assessments without changing the requirements for students and also used the same rubric to grade all assessments. Because this was during the pandemic, I made sure to provide resources and troubleshooting directions if anything happened to the students' devices or if our forum was having technical issues.

Keep in mind that questions that seek analysis are more important than those that only require a summary. This helped students feel a sense of calm instead of anxiety about their assessments. I provided enough time for them to work on the exam and then submit it digitally or physically—whichever was easier for each student group.

Finally, due to the number of posts we created, small-group exercises, and individual papers, it felt like a lot to pack in during such a heavy time for everyone. After listening to student needs and feedback, my colleagues and I decided to eliminate the final exam and instead offer the alternative of doing a group social justice project that they had been preparing for throughout the school year. It was the perfect opportunity to put all their learnings into action and produce a project that would live beyond the classroom. My main priority was to make sure students felt heard; assessments were fair, equitable, and accessible; and every student learned something to apply in their lives.

Assessment techniques fall short when creating sustainable, responsive, and inclusive teaching. Isolating multilingual students and upholding assimilative practices limits linguistic variety and freedom and worsens inequities. We can instead adapt assessments that benefit all students, especially CLDs, by applying anti-racist pedagogy. Students can express their thoughts using their whole language repertoire, and teachers can thoroughly comprehend student understanding in all subject areas. Translanguaging increases engagement and opportunities for meaning-making. It encourages them to utilize self-evaluations and peer-evaluations (see an example in Appendix D), give constructive feedback, use various mediums to present tasks, and show concrete evidence of student understanding. An increasingly diverse country such as the US benefits greatly from the viewpoints that bilingual and multilingual students bring to learning environments, especially schools and classrooms that have been stuck in traditional, White, mainstream English pedagogy that doesn't represent the real world or our students' futures.

HACK 6

DIVERSIFY MATERIALS AND RESOURCES

Integrate Relevant and Supportive Materials

Diverse learning materials and resources promote equity, reduce bias, and create an inclusive learning space for all students. . . . Teachers can create a learning environment that reflects the interests, talents, and experiences of all students in their classroom.
— NATIONAL EDUCATION ASSOCIATION

THE PROBLEM: WE RECYCLE THE SAME EUROCENTRIC THEMES

THERE ARE EDUCATORS who are dedicated to giving students an equitable education. Nevertheless, it's a persistent challenge to determine which method will be the most successful. The Elementary and Secondary Education Act (ESEA) makes it clear that catering to the various requirements of students is not a choice but rather a requirement for schools. Even though conventional curricula continue to privilege the dominant cultures and structures of a monolingual society, it is still the case that racialized students make up a relatively small percentage of the student body, which brings into focus the need to diversify the instructional materials and resources used in schools.

When teachers do not diversify learning materials and resources in K–12 classrooms, it means these classrooms are not being exposed to the full range of perspectives and knowledge that exists in the world. This can lead to an educational system that is not as effective in preparing students for the real world and can lead to students having a limited view of the world. Additionally, this lack of diversity can damage the self-esteem of students of color; they may not feel seen or heard in the classroom. These practices limit the amount of knowledge and understanding that students can gain.

When teachers repeatedly use the same materials and resources, they do not expose students to a variety of perspectives, experiences, and cultures. This can lead to an incomplete understanding of the world and can limit the ability of students to develop critical thinking skills and problem-solving abilities. Additionally, it can lead to a lack of appreciation and understanding of different cultures and experiences.

The colonial influence in US K–12 curriculum resources and materials is pervasive. US history is intricately linked to its colonial past, and this is reflected in many of the materials produced for K–12 students. From textbooks to worksheets, many of the resources touch on the colonial period in some way. For example, many K–12 history textbooks include chapters discussing topics such as the causes of the American Revolution, the impact of the Enlightenment, and the development of the colonies. Additionally, many K–12 math worksheets include questions related to colonial currencies and other colonial-era concepts. Finally, many K–12 literature textbooks contain excerpts from colonial-era authors, such as Benjamin Franklin and Thomas Paine. All of these examples demonstrate the pervasive influence of the colonial period on US K–12 curriculum resources and materials.

THE HACK: DIVERSIFY MATERIALS AND RESOURCES

To combat the little to no representation of CLDs in today's curriculum, we can diversify materials by being intentional with integrating culturally relevant and inclusive content in the classroom and the community. Of course, this hack primarily applies to schools where the teachers can adjust the curriculum, which is not the case in many places. Geneva Gay suggests that culturally responsive education must include a range of pedagogical strategies, such as using culturally appropriate resources and developing fundamental cultural competence abilities. Doing so ensures that teaching and learning materials reflect the backgrounds of learners to reduce cultural misalignment between the home and school contexts.

Using multicultural literature enhances students' self-esteem, interest, engagement, and academic achievement. When teachers use culturally appropriate materials and teaching methods, Black students show higher levels of participation and engagement. Ana María Villegas and Tamara Lucas emphasized the following elements of culturally responsive instruction in their work:

- Understanding how students build their knowledge
- Understanding students' lives
- Sociocultural awareness
- Validating perspectives on diversity
- Implementing diverse teaching methodologies
- Advocating for all students

Use these elements as a guide for diversifying learning materials and resources for your students. When it comes to education, it is especially harmful to ignore or refuse to look into one's own biases. Students need teachers, counselors, administrators, and other stakeholders who put in the time and effort needed to make sure that every student has access to the necessary tools to succeed.

Rethink your curriculum to include more global and historical context and a wide range of perspectives and viewpoints.

We all have some level of implicit and overt bias, whether it's about race or another human quality. As humans, our minds are set up to choose what to accept and what to reject, as long as it aligns with our beliefs and values. Without self-awareness and deliberate action, there is no way to change these ways of thinking, which directly impact our pedagogical practices. We need to distance ourselves from traditional methods that continue to produce the same results if we are ready to champion real change.

In order for social justice initiatives in education to successfully promote diversity and equitable learning, classrooms must endorse CLDs and their communities.

WHAT YOU CAN DO TOMORROW

The traditional US curriculum draws from various aspects of a state's culture, history, and economics, often minimizing culturally and linguistically inclusive policies. Although Common Core standards do not specifically address anti-racism, we can take the initiative and transform learning to build experiences that represent all students and the entire picture of human intellect and accomplishment that includes the contributions of people of all backgrounds. First, we must learn how the curriculum is colonized and why decolonizing it is essential to upholding our pursuit of equitable education. We can find many examples of how colonial efforts are still at play in how systems and structures operate, including the education system. Once you examine how our current methods are influenced by colonialism, you can take steps to implement new methods.

Take into account the wide range of backgrounds represented among your students and ensure that the curriculum includes not only Western but also global perspectives. Rethink your curriculum to include more global and historical context and a wide range of perspectives and viewpoints. Here are a few ideas you can implement right away:

- Research other cultures and countries to gain a better understanding of the diversity of their student populations.
- Incorporate more global perspectives into the curriculum by selecting books, films, and activities that represent different cultures and backgrounds.
- Invite guest speakers to the classroom to share their perspectives and experiences.
- Ask students to share their own cultural experiences, highlighting similarities and differences.
- Encourage students to explore different cultures on their own, either through reading, watching films, or interacting with members of other cultures in the community.

- Incorporate classroom activities that involve working in teams and collaborating with members of different backgrounds.
- Participate in cultural events in the community, such as festivals and celebrations, and involve your students or incorporate related class projects when possible.
- Explore different cultures through technology in the classroom, such as virtual reality or online videos.
- Encourage discussion among students to ensure that everyone is comfortable sharing their perspectives.
- Foster an inclusive environment in the classroom by creating a space where all students feel safe to express their ideas.

A BLUEPRINT FOR FULL IMPLEMENTATION

STEP 1: **Become aware of how your school contributes to maintaining colonial power systems.**

Be on the lookout for and question practices that may appear convenient but ultimately put students at risk. Rethink and adopt new strategies to benefit your school, your students, and the overall community. Ideas include:

- Research the history of the school, including its founding and its relationship to the local community.
- Examine the school's policies and curriculum for any connections to colonial power systems.

- Talk to students, parents, and school staff to get their perspectives on the school's practices and the power dynamics within it.

- Engage in conversations with the staff and faculty about how their work contributes to colonial power systems.

- Read and discuss scholarly research on colonialism and its impacts on education systems.

- Attend workshops and conferences related to anticolonial education.

- Advocate for broader structural changes, such as equitable funding and decolonized hiring practices.

STEP 2: Decolonize the curriculum.

To provide a better and more inclusive educational experience for all students by decolonizing the curriculum, you need to perform a thorough reevaluation, reframing, and reconstruction of the current curriculum. The goal is to broaden our criteria of quality literature so that we stop celebrating a single point of view and pushing the dominant narrative.

Examine the current curriculum and determine which content to remove or update. Identify topics and readings that center the colonial narrative, and identify ways to reframe the material to be more inclusive and diverse. Incorporate the perspectives of Indigenous peoples and other marginalized communities into the curriculum. Do this through readings, lectures, and course activities. You can broaden the scope of the course to include more non-Western perspectives by introducing new texts, authors, and topics that challenge the Western-centric narrative. When we encourage students to critically engage with traditional course materials by introducing different ways of thinking and approaching the material, we create a safe learning environment where students can openly discuss and challenge the colonial narrative. This allows students to develop their understanding of the material and ask questions that may challenge the traditional narrative. Regularly update the course and frequently introduce new materials to keep up with changing perspectives and ideas. (Work with Indigenous and other marginalized communities to ensure that you decolonize the curriculum with respect and dignity.)

Note: Creating a curriculum that is welcoming to all students requires a diverse reading selection. However, it does not overtly combat racism or engage the student in the idea of decolonization.

STEP 3: Collaboratively build classroom materials with your students.

Students can help you examine the appropriate sources to choose from while you build your classroom curriculum. For resources on where to start, check out Tolerance Education: Research-Based Methods for Anti-Racism Training, and similar options that offer suggestions for combating racism and prejudice in the classroom. You can find examples in Appendix E.1 and E.2.

STEP 4: Find out what students already think about diversity.

During the class discussion, use the brave space method to challenge those ideas. Reading aloud together and having a conversation about the works of writers from various ethnic backgrounds is an excellent way to attain this goal for students of any age. Students in elementary school, and even those in higher grades, can learn a lot from picture books, especially students who are visual learners. Ask your colleagues for recommendations, read top books on the subject, or curate materials from various cultures for your classroom library.

STEP 5: Challenge the status quo.

As you examine your school's role in reproducing colonial ideologies and practices, you can take the initiative and push for change. If you serve in a more restrictive environment, it helps to present this approach to some students but not all. Teaching students individually rather than using a cookie-cutter curriculum is ideal. Use decolonization's tenets of wholeness, agency, growth, introspection, and communal connection to validate students' perspectives.

These approaches help students develop their own identities rather than forcing them to blend in. Provide customized learning experiences. For example, you can plan a trip to the museum for a group of students to learn about their history, develop projects around that trip, and loop in their parents and guardians. Collaborate with other educators to make this process smooth and sustainable.

OVERCOMING PUSHBACK

The topic of diversifying classroom materials and resources lends itself to so many questions that could be perceived as pushback. However, it's a great opportunity to share a positive message in the way you respond and to bring parents, educators, and administrators on board with these life-changing initiatives.

I don't have a diverse classroom, so I don't need to "diversify" materials. That's even more of a reason to diversify your classroom! Students who live in places without much or any diversity might benefit more from explicit lessons on diversity. These students may lack the experiences they need to challenge their preconceived notions about people outside of their communities.

I do not see color; we are all the same, so I teach my students to promote unity by not seeing color. This is a problematic statement. When people make such a statement or lead with this thought process, they often do so with the intention of fostering unity rather than conflict. But people who say this often also worry that learning about different points of view could cause students and teachers to disagree with each other. Even parents may express this concern. So, pretending we are all the same instead of celebrating what makes us unique doesn't teach students how to deal with the real differences in worldviews that exist, nor does it help them understand other people or teach them about social justice. If the goal is to help students see others for who they truly are and not treat them differently, then they need to understand the value of diversity and get along well with people from different backgrounds.

I don't acknowledge specific cultural celebrations, traditions, or practices because no one brings them to my attention. Invite your students to share an important celebration or tradition they must partake in so you are aware and can use that information to support them appropriately. It is important for you to acknowledge and respect diverse holidays in the classroom to show respect toward all students and their diverse backgrounds. (If your school allows for such lessons.) This can help create an inclusive environment and help students feel valued and respected. It can also foster an understanding and appreciation of different cultures and build relationships between students of different backgrounds. Acknowledging and respecting diverse holidays can be an important part of educating students on cultural diversity and raising awareness of different cultures.

My subject is not directly related to social justice or diversity, so it will be challenging to incorporate those concepts into my classroom. Our students' identities and experiences reflect the real world. Relate what they are learning to the real world, which makes it related to social justice—whether it's math, science, or English. For example, connect mathematical concepts to social justice issues. When teaching about the power of exponential growth, discuss how the compounding of wealth over time can lead to inequality; when teaching about data analysis and graphing, use stories from different cultural perspectives to help students understand the data. For science, you could provide readings or videos about scientists from diverse backgrounds and guide the students to discuss their findings.

I do not feel comfortable teaching about other communities I do not belong in. I prefer someone from that group to teach about their community instead. If we all held off until we had a greater demographic representation of individuals from various backgrounds before addressing the issue of diverse instructional materials in the classroom, the work would never move forward. This is necessary work that calls for every teacher to ensure that students are properly educated and have access to the right resources and information in their learning. Your efforts to include diverse materials and presentations are certainly better than none. Consider opportunities for professional development in this area, as well as resources from the library, community groups, or non-profit organization websites focused on social justice.

I am afraid to offend my students. What if I say or do the wrong thing? That is a completely valid and normal question. It can be hard to know how to infuse the right resources into the classroom. You can begin by including resources that are already accessible within your school community. One best practice is to talk to invested parents, guardians, other teachers, and other adults in the community. This also takes the pressure off students who usually take on the role of unpaid sherpas by being put on the spot to answer questions about their communities, assuming that they are an "expert" on their own culture. Additionally, some organizations make resources and other materials available online to the education community. These websites are great places to learn more about how to diversify the curriculum, which will naturally make you feel more comfortable tackling diverse topics.

THE HACK IN ACTION

In the summer of 2022, Ms. Irvin planned cultural engagements for a group of her students, Black girls in sixth through eighth grade, that went beyond "traditional" boundaries. From pulling in the community to training students to practice positive affirmations and chants, from learning about Black girlhood and sisterhood to playing culturally relevant games, these activities built stronger relationships and a close-knit classroom culture. She infused technology as well and made sure to include platforms and activities that her students were already interested in or were familiar with.

Ms. Irvin organized a program for young Black girls and wanted them to learn about sisterhood. She sent out the following letter to invite Black women to spend time with Black girls:

Hey Schola Sistas,

Thank you for being willing to come hang with the girls tomorrow. All summer we have engaged in all things Black girlhood through discussion, expression, and playing team-building games like Breaking Bread. The goal of tomorrow's hangout will be to talk about sisterhood in all its forms for Black women and girls. I've broken this up into parts.

Part A: I would love it if you all began with a discussion on how you define sisterhood. What does it mean to you? I would like to have the girls understand the meaning of sorority, the significance of the Divine 9 and sisterhood orgs within, which sisterhood you are part of, and whatever else is driven by the discussion.

Part B: Next, we'll split up into small groups for a more intimate conversation with the girls. The following are loose guiding questions that I will put on the board for these smaller group discussions.

- ▶ What does sisterhood mean?
- ▶ What does sisterhood do for us?
- ▶ How does it support and challenge us?
- ▶ Why is it important to them/us. How is it developed? Identified?

Part C: We generally like to materialize or create as a way to show and share our takeaways. I'll have the girls translate their small-group discussion onto posters they will design together and later share. You may stay for this if time allows, but feel free to dip out if you have other obligations.

Lunch/Break

Know and Remember Ritual

Thank you,

Ms. Irvin

Watching her build this experience from scratch was inspiring. She put her heart into creating it, collaborating with colleagues and, of course, including student input based on feedback before finalizing the entire curriculum. She applied a backward design, first identifying what her students would need. From a student-centered approach, she designed experiences that would support human connection and promote personal growth and development. You may want to consider this approach as you bring in the community and engage them with the classroom. It allows for inclusion and collaboration in often overlooked ways.

When there is a mismatch between lessons and home cultures, students can struggle to find their identity. They may not have the same values and beliefs as their peers. They may feel misunderstood and like they don't belong in either place. They may also feel confused or conflicted about which values and beliefs to embrace and which to reject. This process can be especially difficult for students who come from diverse backgrounds, as they may feel like they must choose between different cultures or parts of their identity. Ultimately, the process of trying to find their identity can be a source of stress and confusion for many students. As educators, we can help by putting careful thought into our curriculum, class materials, and resources to ensure they are diverse and relevant.

DESIGN LEARNING EXPERIENCES BEYOND THE CLASSROOM

Connect Learning to Lived Experiences, Historical Events, and the Future

Designing learning experiences that extend beyond the classroom can provide students with opportunities to practice their skills, work together in teams, and gain invaluable insights into the real-world application of their knowledge.
— NICOLE LEGATE, EDUCATION CONSULTANT

THE PROBLEM: STUDENTS CANNOT CONNECT THEIR EXPERIENCES TO THEIR LEARNING

DUE TO OUTDATED education approaches, it can be challenging for students to connect history with current events and to understand their positionality in the world. Learning should be designed to prepare students for life. In the information age, we can collaboratively create a world economy in which we can all thrive by sharing real-life knowledge. The power of connectivity is changing the very nature of learning as education and technology work together to give students new ways to make connections and share ideas. During the industrial age, education was based on a one-size-fits-all model, but that clearly is not a recipe for success for students of today.

Naturally, sticking with what we already know is easier than trying new methods, which is why we often fear change in education. However, plenty of evidence exists that the education culture has to change. This is not only an issue in the US, as other parts of the world experience a similar situation, especially formerly colonized nations.

I remember a running joke when I was in Uganda; we used to laugh because several generations of my family used the exact same textbook, with writings on the old pages that were holding on for dear life. Ignorantly, I thought I would not find a similar issue in the US, but I learned that students are still assigned to read the same "classics" such as *To Kill a Mockingbird, Romeo and Juliet,* and *The Great Gatsby.* Most of these books are not culturally and linguistically accessible to all students. Although many educators appreciate the longevity of these titles, students crave to learn from both old and new materials that they can connect to generationally and culturally.

> *Help students comprehend global injustices and encourage them to take action in the areas they are passionate about, whether in small or big ways.*

Another common issue is how history continues to be told from a White perspective when, in fact, newer information shows contradicting facts that change everything for students. Did Christopher Columbus truly discover America? Were slaves truly freed on July 4, 1776? If so, then why are we officially celebrating Juneteenth as of 2021? Is "Thanksgiving" truly about giving thanks and peace? Why are books about racism, gender, and romantic relationships being banned? Why is there a heavy push to ban The 1619 Project? I could continue, but the need for change is clear.

THE HACK: DESIGN LEARNING EXPERIENCES BEYOND THE CLASSROOM

What would happen if today's teachers strove to provide their students with the learning experiences that help them gain the skills they need to survive in a world that is changing so quickly? When teachers work together with the community, they can collectively create engaging materials and resources, plus relevant opportunities that motivate students to take action. By combining critical technology perspectives with culturally diverse digital and print resources in support of social justice-focused education, we concurrently build diverse literacies in our curricula. For example, librarians, community leaders, parents, and social studies teachers can work together to lay the groundwork for students to actively participate in service-learning projects and global activities. This allows everyone to be part of the change they want to see in their communities by actively identifying societal injustices such as those caused by racism, sexism, heterocentrism, ableism, and classism.

Students and teachers experience several advantages when learning occurs outside of the traditional classroom norms and settings. When you create opportunities for students to put their classroom knowledge into practice in the real world, it creates a more engaging and effective learning environment that also encourages students' personal and social growth. Students who become involved in extracurricular activities report feeling more motivated, remembering more of the course information, and doing better academically overall. When using this approach to create equitable learning experiences, always keep in mind that well-structured lessons help students comprehend global injustices and encourage them to take action in the areas they are passionate about, whether in small or big ways, and the impact is long-lasting.

WHAT YOU CAN DO TOMORROW

To design learning beyond the classroom, we must bring social justice into the classroom too. Consider adopting the Social Justice Standards, which serve as an Antibias Framework for instruction. According to Learning for Justice, the framework provides anchor standards and appropriate grade-level learning outcomes organized around four areas: **Identity, Diversity, Justice, and Action (IDJA).** You can use them to guide or inform your curriculum development so that it fosters more equity and accessibility for all students.

Learning for Justice created the IDJA standards to help educators foster inclusive, equitable, and affirming classrooms. The standards provide guidance on topics such as recognizing and responding to the intersectionality of identities, understanding power and privilege, and taking action to promote justice. Each of the four sections contains specific learning objectives, activities, and resources to help educators implement the standards in their classrooms. Visit their website to dive deeper and explore more resources. Keep an eye open for a model IDJA lesson I created in Appendix F.1. The following ideas can help you get started on implementing learning experiences beyond the classroom.

- **Consider your answers to these questions as you incorporate real-world experiences and events into your curriculum:** How do I define myself? What makes us who we are? How are our identities today shaped by society? Do the ways we identify ourselves change over time? How do different parts of our identities combine to make us who we are? Does how we present our identities change depending on where we are or the people we are with?

- **Assign cultural concoctions.** Instruct students to create and present their own cultural concoction (drawing, painting, video, written piece, interview, or documentary) about three characteristics that define them. This should include aspects of their social identity, which you can arrange in an easily accessible and shareable format. Start by discussing your identity, demonstrating self-awareness and reflection. You can use this approach in the arts, social sciences, and STEAM classes to help students learn about the complexity of social identity (a social construct) and the fact that identities can coexist and lead to intersections between different forms or systems of oppression, dominance, or discrimination. Social identity intricacies are always at play. When you adopt an intersectionality lens in your practice, you afford students the ability to understand the complexities of identities and how they shape our lived experiences in the past, present, and future.

- **Make real-life connections in all your teaching.** By linking what students are studying to their lives and circumstances, you motivate them to care about what they are learning. For example, in a language arts class, you may assign readings about current events that impact students. Making a direct connection between the learning and their daily experiences helps students feel that their teachers care about them. Motivate students to think about how they can identify issues within their communities and create solutions with their peers.

A BLUEPRINT FOR FULL IMPLEMENTATION

STEP 1: Consider the Universal Design for Learning (UDL).

UDL is an education paradigm that helps teachers facilitate learning throughout the student experience, and it increases accessibility to all lessons. The National Center for Universal Design for Learning provides many resources for teachers. UDL includes three primary brain networks in the learning process: the *recognition network* (emphasizes the importance of providing multiple options for recognizing student achievement), the *strategy network* (allows students to access and use the strategies they need to be successful and has three components: Engagement, Representation, and Action & Expression), and the *emotional network* (focuses on the idea that students learn best when they are in a safe, supportive environment and when their emotional needs are met). To effectively use UDL in the classroom, teachers must first have a firm grasp of the underlying principles and neural networks of UDL. The likelihood of early academic success is significantly influenced by the teacher's clarity and transparency about their expectations.

STEP 2: Encourage students to use tools and features they are comfortable with and to try new ones.

If you assigned the cultural concoctions activity as described in the What You Can Do Tomorrow section, give each student three to five minutes to present their final creative work and discuss their options for using familiar tools and features or new ones. For example, they may want to use a new tool to create a visual description of how they believe others perceive them. Ask them if they learned anything new about their classmates or themselves. Provide time to reflect on how their cultural identity affects their decisions, actions, and beliefs, and conclude with a journal-writing session or roundtable discussion.

STEP 3: Take a physical or digital virtual reality tour.

To curate diverse learning resources and materials, take a tour! For example, bring a librarian into the classroom so they can instruct students on how to navigate sources, determine the credibility of information, and develop research skills. As students acquire these skills, they can include nontraditional resources such as digital books, podcasts, websites, virtual libraries, and virtual museums. At the end, students should know how to critique a resource and provide constructive feedback; evaluate the credibility of a source based on who, what, why, how, and when; accurately cite sources using the appropriate formats; collect and analyze information on specific topics; gain an understanding of both familiar and unfamiliar subjects; and critically consider and construct convincing arguments and opinions.

STEP 4: Establish a collaborative classroom culture.

Through peer teaching, students educate one another by resolving misconceptions and eradicating assumptions. It is also a great strategy that prepares them for life beyond primary school; collaboration is a vital skill for all students to learn.

In smaller groups, divide students into pairs to discuss a particular assignment. Clearly define and describe the activity objectives. In larger groups, appoint someone to record the notes and speak on the group's behalf. Students are more likely to stay engaged when they have a responsibility in a group activity. Offer adequate time to complete the assignment and make yourself available to answer questions. When you collectively debrief, ask the designated speakers to share a summary of their conversation. Answer questions and clear up any myths and ambiguities.

STEP 5: Prioritize students' academic success through authentic connections and inclusive strategies.

Roselle Chartock, author of *Strategies and Lessons for Culturally Responsive Teaching*, suggested the following pedagogical strategies to improve inclusive teaching: Believe that every student has something to share with the class in the form of personal stories (such as counter-narratives) and experiences. Encourage students to recognize their similarities and differences regarding their past, present, and other experiences. Give every student, regardless of color, religion, ethnicity, gender, class, or ability, an equal opportunity to reach their potential. Decorate the classroom with inclusive visuals the students will recognize and relate to. Uphold compassionate connections, and refrain from forming assumptions about racial or ethnic groups and the sources of their cultural traits and customs. Talk with students about the fact that people belonging to the same group might vary greatly from one another (which calls for intersectionality discussions with your students).

STEP 6: Design fun and meaningful learning experiences.

The world can be a scary place, and bringing that world into the classroom can be a challenge to keep positive. Your lesson ideas should pique the students' interest, encourage them to use their imagination, and propel them into independent study. Include students in the process of creating lessons. Through technology and gamification, you can create a more personal relationship with your students and eliminate management issues in the classroom. Cross-pollinating their love of games with learning will help them love learning as well!

OVERCOMING PUSHBACK

Here are a couple of responses you may want to use when you hear pushback about your efforts to design learning experiences beyond the classroom.

We don't need to make everything about social justice, especially learning. It's true: not all lessons focus directly on social justice. Rather, they can integrate aspects of social justice in some way to ensure students feel supported in a safe, welcoming environment. We must examine why we do not think it is reasonable to acknowledge the societal issues that affect our racialized students and colleagues, inside and outside the classroom. When teachers make sure students are seen and heard and their experiences are welcomed in the classroom, the students will be more likely to engage, which may increase their academic performance. To become culturally inclusive educators, we must include real societal (and age-appropriate) issues and experiences in our classrooms.

I don't want to make some students feel uncomfortable or develop negative feelings. First, consider racialized students, who often are not mentally (or in other ways) protected from the painful reality of our society. It helps to put yourself in their shoes and rethink the way you approach your discussions surrounding social justice issues. The intention is not to point fingers or blame students for the historical and contemporary events that have affected racialized communities for far too long. Instead, it is to open a dialogue about how we can understand others and work together on dismantling oppressive systems and structures. Always evaluate the root of your concerns and consider how your racialized students and colleagues feel when it's considered "taboo" to learn about their reality in class.

THE HACK IN ACTION

In spring 2020, I taught a required social justice (social studies) class, originally designed by Dr. Gutierrez, a professor of curriculum and instruction in Latina/Latino studies, and whose research investigates the intersections of race, class, and language on classroom dynamics in the field of mathematics education. We engaged in many conversations about social justice topics. It wasn't always easy to engage students, especially at first, and we had a few moments where I questioned my ability to be vulnerable with my students because it conflicted with my identity as a Black immigrant woman and my role as their teacher, especially because of the questions one student asked me at the beginning of the pandemic:

> *"Does Africa have developed technology? How are they dealing with COVID? Why aren't they reporting accurate numbers of COVID deaths?"*

It was shocking to me, hearing those questions. I did not have an immediate response, and I also did not want to portray myself as a spokesperson for the entire continent of Africa just because I'd shared with the class that I am an African immigrant as part of an identity activity. In that moment, I remembered that I was creating a brave space, so I had to welcome such questions and address them with a collected mind. For racialized teachers, it can be challenging to navigate social justice topics with our students when our lived experiences are so painful—like the week of George Floyd's murder. We still had to show up and make space to grapple with the different realities, regardless of students' identities and opinions—or whatever questions they asked.

As I taught this course, the murder of George Floyd and the events that followed were still very fresh. In addition, the ongoing anti-Blackness in Asia and the anti-Asian events in the US were exploding due to the pandemic. Several negative events were happening in real time, which made this class particularly unique— training future teachers to unpack current events and asking them to build learning experiences for their peers while helping them cultivate skills to facilitate such conversations in their future classrooms. Over time, we reflected on a social justice reading through classroom discussions, group presentations, and discussion boards. Later in the project, I broke the class up into small groups so they could start developing their final group projects. My intention was that they would build vocabulary and knowledge to help with their final projects, which I wanted them to design as a digital product they could share with the community.

The project was for three or four students to conduct research that focused on a social justice topic, then design a technology-based project addressing that issue (most students chose projects about misconceptions, stereotypes, or ideologies held in society), and conclude by recommending an educational solution. They were to build their final products and showcase them in front of the class and then plan a resource launch event that would engage their families, friends, and the larger community. The main goals were for others to unlearn or to challenge common misconceptions, stereotypes, or ideologies about students and education, as well as share resources and knowledge about impactful solutions to address social injustice. Group grades relied on the quality, accuracy, delivery, and completion of their final projects. They would also receive peer feedback, which helped to hold each other accountable and created an opportunity for me to gauge how much each student contributed to the project. My students showcased thought-provoking projects that incorporated different kinds of technology and media. You can find a social justice project assessment in Appendix F.2.

This chapter addressed the fact that some educators still adhere to the antiquated notion that in order to prepare students for the real world, they should train students to listen, refrain from asking questions, and repeatedly memorize. Due to this old way of thinking, it becomes difficult for students to link history and contemporary events—to comprehend their place in society. One purpose of education should be to prepare students for real life and the workplace, and another, among many, is for students to love and enjoy learning. In the digital age, our economy is built on the cooperative creation of a world in which we may all flourish. With the help of educational technology, students now have more opportunities than ever to collaborate, form relationships, and exchange ideas. If our students are to acquire the skills they need to live in a world that is changing so fast, today's teachers must focus on giving students equitable, quality experiences. When educators collaborate with the community, they raise the chance of providing resources and learning experiences that are relevant to students' lives and inspire them to take action.

EVALUATE YOUR CULTURAL COMPETENCE

Conduct Ongoing Self-Assessments and Reflections

Culturally competent educators are those who recognize the importance of understanding and respecting cultural differences and strive to create an inclusive environment in which all students can reach their full potential.
— **National Education Association**

THE PROBLEM: EDUCATORS DON'T RECOGNIZE THEIR OWN ATTITUDES TOWARD CULTURAL DIFFERENCES

THE CONCEPT OF cultural competence emerged in the 1980s in the fields of social work and counseling psychology. Relevant to education and teaching strategies, it is the possession and application of knowledge and skills in four areas: awareness of one's own cultural worldview, recognition of one's attitudes toward cultural differences, awareness of different cultural practices, and thoughtfulness in cross-cultural interaction. In contrast, White people have generally been given the benefit of the doubt when it comes to interpreting our nation's historical narratives, beliefs, values, regulations, and legislative acts.

In recent years, we have seen a rise in the number of films, documentaries, and mobile phone videos providing evidence of issues that many thought were long gone, and others argue that this evidence has "divided" the country. Regarding education, adequate records of educational inequalities exist in schools, further proving why we need to increase the cultural competency of teachers. Teachers with cultural competence create learning environments that support diversity, inclusivity, and democracy in larger communities.

THE HACK: EVALUATE YOUR CULTURAL COMPETENCE

The National Education Association states that due to the increasingly diverse student body in PK–12 education, teachers should be culturally competent. Culture is important for learning because it promotes better teaching, helps close assumed achievement disparities among students, and aids teachers in upholding accountability. Additionally, educators are better able to communicate with students' families and maintain democracy. Social movements such as Black Lives Matter and Stop Asian Hate have emerged in recent years to address racial injustices, discrimination, violence, and other forms of social destruction.

Many communities are advocating for more transformational and justice-focused curricula in schools. Because these issues are so close to home and spread so prevalently in communities, education stakeholders will witness a shift in student engagement when these efforts are successful.

To benefit your students and foster an inclusive environment, you must confront your personal fears—such as not wanting to talk about racial or social justice issues, worries about being called out as racists or privileged, feelings of vulnerability, and prejudices in a brave space environment. In order to provide equitable learning, you must amplify the voices of historically silenced students, ensuring that no student is invisible. To create and facilitate environments that embrace multicultural education, come prepared and equipped with the appropriate tools.

Teachers need to understand the pervasiveness of racism and other forms of bias in our society and how their own cultural values and beliefs shape their work with students.

According to best practices shared by teachers across the United States, there is a strong relationship between culturally competent teachers and positive student outcomes. Data shows that over 80 percent of public school teachers are White, a percentage that has remained constant over the last twenty years, highlighting the underrepresentation of racialized educators. As a solution, we must create and implement cultural competency evaluations with a focus on intersectionality and also include student versions to triangulate results. Students who anonymously assess their teachers' cultural competence will provide solid input and open opportunities to consider the variety of perspectives and perceptions that such a cultural competence evaluation could generate.

WHAT YOU CAN DO TOMORROW

To become culturally competent, teachers need to understand the pervasiveness of racism and other forms of bias in our society and how their own cultural values and beliefs shape their work with students. They need to realize they can change institutional procedures to improve educational opportunities for all students. They can champion equity, demonstrate an ability to work effectively with students and others from diverse backgrounds, and disrupt injustice by working to dismantle inequitable pedagogical practices that impede access and opportunity. To show your students that you are intentional about including their cultural, emotional, and intellectual needs and want to promote cultural awareness in the classroom, you need to create a plan in action, starting with working on yourself.

To do this, you can employ a plethora of strategies to establish solid relationships with all your students, especially racialized students and low-income students, who are frequently more vulnerable in our society. To strategically reflect on your pedagogical practices and create a culturally aware environment and equitable instruction, consider the following questions: Does your teaching take into account the diverse cultural and linguistic backgrounds, skills, and knowledge of your students? Does your current approach support the academic, social, emotional, cultural, psychological, and physical health of your students? How do you get parents, caregivers, leaders/organizers, and other community members to engage in different stages of the process? Do you teach in a way that helps students link what they're learning to their daily experiences or communities?

You can deepen your cultural competence by incorporating these activities into your practice right away.

- **Critically examine how cultural worldviews influence your perceptions of power, dominance, and inequality.** Take a look at how views on any subject vary from culture to culture. For example, some cultures may view power, dominance, and inequality as a positive and necessary part of life, while other cultures may view them as oppressive and unjust. Furthermore, consider how these cultural beliefs shape and influence the way we perceive power, dominance, and inequality in our own lives. For example, if a culture places a strong emphasis on hierarchical power structures, then it is likely that individuals will view power, dominance, and inequality in a more traditional sense. On the other hand, if a culture places a greater emphasis on egalitarianism, individuals may view power, dominance, and inequality in a more progressive manner. It is also essential to consider how cultural worldviews interact with other social factors, such as gender, race, class, and sexuality, which can further shape our perceptions of power, dominance, and inequality.

  To build an inclusive classroom, you must carefully consider your views and beliefs via thoughtful questions and in-depth group discussions.

Because of our upbringing and experiences, we develop certain beliefs and viewpoints. These often depend on unproven assumptions. When pursuing cultural competency, prepare to reflect based on your views and the way you think. Through ongoing reflection, you can learn about and discover the experiences of other cultural groups, consider how your perspectives compare to those of others, and ultimately raise your socio-cultural consciousness and work toward dismantling oppressive and biased systems.

To expand your expertise, you must discover the relevant materials and tools. Consider what facts, events, or settings shape your values. Open-mindedly and willingly inquire about the basis of others' views, too. Examining and criticizing your views and values teaches you about the complexities of not just your cultural framework but also those of others (your students, their parents, and your colleagues). This aptitude will help you teach students from different cultures more effectively and allow you to tap more deeply into your understanding of yourself.

- **Show that you care about your students' identities beyond their race or culture.** Students are more likely to be vulnerable to teachers who are genuinely interested in their backgrounds. Naturally, humans like to feel seen, heard, and understood. Taking an interest in your students beyond their cultural backgrounds helps to form relationships and creates a better learning experience. Consider starting a conversation about students' futures. What do they want to do? How can they get there? What barriers exist? Ask them about their talents and skills and find creative ways to leverage that information in their learning or with particular projects. Encourage students to discuss current events that matter to them. If certain students are passionate about social justice issues like immigration, the environment, women's rights, the law, or LGBTQ2+, you can teach them how to research topics independently and engage in critical discourse, regardless of your or other students' points of view.

- **Diversify your knowledge and expand your networks.** Consider attending conferences, working with other teachers to share and gain knowledge, and trying out different methods of consuming information as part of your professional development as a teacher who is attentive to and supportive of students' CLDs. This self-education might include watching videos, listening to podcasts and audiobooks, and even keeping a journal. We have the tools and technology to build professional networks and share and learn from a wide range of colleagues, including using social media networks and education platforms. Take advantage of your favorite ways to connect and collaborate as you diversify your knowledge and incorporate critical thinking and social justice into your teaching.

- **Take cultural competency surveys that emphasize intersectionality.** To include, value, and hear CLDs in our classrooms, we must intentionally apply an intersectional lens and make space for authentic resources and materials that represent the world more accurately. This means including everyone equally, beyond the traditional emphasis on White, binary, English-speaking, cisgender, able-bodied, male, middle- and upper-class, and Eurocentric students. Understanding your cultural competence can dramatically transform your teaching and provide opportunities for you to create the kind of classroom that reflects the real world while preparing students for it. To make progress along the cultural competence continuum, you will shift your thinking from accepting diversity to fostering change for social justice. Most people are somewhere between cultural incompetence and cultural blindness. Every teacher can benefit from a self-evaluation to see where they are now and where they want to be. You may also want to ask students for their feedback about your cultural competency, and you will gain wisdom by reading their responses and contrasting them with your own.

  You can find cultural competence surveys online or see an alternative example in Appendix G.1.

- **Encourage diverse viewpoints and interactions.** Which students' voices are heard the most in your classroom? How are you amplifying students who do not normally speak up? Whose narratives do you tell? Most US teaching materials tend to focus on Western, White, male, and middle-class stories. Do you incorporate diverse ideas into the curriculum? Are you including books written by CLD authors? Examine historical narratives to see which voices are missing and begin to include them.

A BLUEPRINT FOR FULL IMPLEMENTATION

STEP 1: Do the internal work.

Acts that are only on the outside are performative, and we cannot solve the root of the issues if we skip the internal work. Use the strategies and tools provided in Dr. Vernita Mayfield's book *Cultural Competence Now: 56 Exercises to Help Educators Understand and Challenge Bias, Racism, and Privilege* to prepare you to discuss urgent and uncomfortable social justice issues. She explores the four parts of the self-evaluation process.

- *Awaken and Evaluate.* Improve your cultural competence, knowledge, and abilities by evaluating your values and beliefs and how they materialize in your actions. Inequity has historical roots, and you must acknowledge this and prepare to confront those origins.

- *Apply and Act.* Follow the initial step, then adjust your pedagogy.

- *Analyze and Align.* Dismantle inequitable policies and align resources to promote essential adjustments to institutionalize equality practices in the classroom.

- *Advocate and Lead.* Learn the skills, knowledge, and attitudes required for your role as a leader and equity champion.

Additionally, work on the phases of the cultural competence continuum. It will help you better understand different cultures and their values, beliefs, and practices so you can meet the needs of your students. This helps you create an inclusive, equitable learning environment that allows all students to feel accepted and respected, leading to improved student engagement and academic outcomes. Additionally, understanding the cultural competence continuum can help you recognize and address any potential biases or prejudices in your teaching, which can help you create a more positive learning environment. You will find the four phases of the continuum in Appendix G.2.

STEP 2: "See" your students and pronounce their full names correctly.

Ensure that each student in the class feels welcomed and included. The simplest ways to demonstrate this are to know everyone's name and to welcome each student to class. I emphasize knowing the students' names and pronouncing them correctly because names are a huge part of their identities. Do not offer them a nickname or an "easier" way to pronounce their names. Building trust begins with little gestures that demonstrate you care about your students. Ask students to teach you how they pronounce their names, or make a quick phone call to the parents before school starts. Any culturally competent educator would not want to make their students uncomfortable. However, if teachers don't make an effort to pronounce their students' names properly, those students are more likely to feel disregarded. Take extra steps to break down the phonics of the name in writing or next to the attendance sheet and include the same details on attendance sheets for substitute teachers. Practice, practice, practice!

STEP 3: Be approachable.

The smallest details can make it difficult for students to connect with you. You want them to feel comfortable coming to you and asking questions. Make it clear that they may come to you with issues or just to say hello, and then address questions they bring to you. Be aware of your posture, language, tone, and facial expressions. Walk around the room checking in on students instead of sitting behind the desk all the time. Pause during lessons and allow students to ask questions before you move on. You can screen the room for any confused faces and give enough transition time. Consider an open-door policy for office hours or one-on-ones. Some students are more comfortable in private, or they may feel afraid to ask questions during the lessons. Provide a safe space for open dialogue.

STEP 4: Value language and cultural diversity.

Encourage diverse linguistic ways of practice and ensure that non-native speakers have access to educational resources that are appropriate for their level of English proficiency. CLDs often feel excluded, misunderstood, and under pressure to suppress their native tongue in favor of English in non-culturally-inclusive classrooms. Consider whether you have internalized raciolinguistic ideologies, which are restrictive viewpoints on language and racialization. For example, criticizing or policing how people speak in order to conform to standards or norms, or discriminating against people for their accent or dialect. In education, these raciolinguistic ideologies are deeply rooted in the policies that inform pedagogy. Examine your internalized ideologies, and adjust them accordingly. Normalize a more nuanced understanding of the world by personally reading literature produced by culturally and linguistically diverse and racialized writers who have documented contemporary and historical events and their personal experiences. Also encourage students to incorporate that literature in their projects, and it's even better if the material exists in their home languages.

OVERCOMING PUSHBACK

Your efforts to improve your cultural competence will pay off for you and your students, but you may have to pause and answer questions like these from other educators and stakeholders.

What if leadership does not support this approach or provide cultural competency training? This is a valid and urgent concern in education because a gap exists in teacher training when it comes to cultural competency. It is a multilayered issue that needs to be addressed on several levels, but as an individual, you can take the initiative by doing the internal work, being vulnerable with trusted colleagues, and asking for help. You can also take the extra step and push hard on your leadership to make this a priority for your school and district. This work can be less intimidating when you have a community of practice to lean on and support from leadership, but the lack of those supports should not get in the way of your personal growth.

Cultural competency programs are time-consuming and expensive. Of course, ideally, leadership would invest in these learning opportunities. Regardless, through collaboration with other educators, you can create free and accessible mini trainings or start a shared document of free resources. Ask leadership to allow you the time to gather resources and to participate in learning and development opportunities.

I am afraid others will isolate or target me due to my cultural competence efforts. You are not alone. Teachers who try to bring about change and challenge the status quo likely feel alone and unsupported. Others may feel the same as you but are afraid to express their concerns. Stand firm in your beliefs and values and know that you, as an educator, have the power to drive change—especially now. Students need you to advocate for change in the educational system. Request support in ways that you need and deserve. Be aware that you can advocate for yourself, too, if you are targeted due to your interest in cultural competency.

THE HACK IN ACTION

I have done a lot of reflecting in the past fourteen years, even before I became an educator. Although I identify as a Black woman, I have had to learn so much about what that means for me, specifically in the US. Being a Black immigrant added a unique perspective and experience of what being Black means, which also revealed that I had much to learn about my positionality in different spaces. I have unpacked my identity complexities because being Black is richly diverse. It is not a monolith—we do not all walk and talk the same way, we do not all look or dress the same, and we absolutely do not all have the same beliefs or values. Also, just because a Black person is perceived as "different" from whatever societal expectations are for Black persons, it does not make them "better" or "worse" than other Black people. It's the beauty of being unique in our Blackness.

Admittedly, as a child, I only saw stereotypical images of Black people in the US. That is what Ugandan television exposes many Africans to, and I am positive that it is the same situation today across the continent. This leads to many people believing these stereotypes and acting on them. The media is powerful and influential in how they portray certain groups of people. I can give many examples of how Black people have been the victims of hate crimes based on the color of their skin. These acts of racism take root in deep hate, stereotyping, and other issues.

In education, we have many examples of how racialized students have been "left behind" because some teachers deemed them unteachable or just "difficult" to discipline. Many factors are getting in the way of teachers truly connecting and understanding these CLDs: cultural differences, preconceived notions, and an unwillingness to reflect and change. As a Black immigrant and now educator, I had to unlearn false beliefs that the media and other sources taught me, even about my identity (language and culture).

I became comfortable with having difficult conversations with my friends, family, and colleagues, and even strangers, about how our thoughts and beliefs influence our actions and how we treat others. High school was a particular turning point for me. I was already fighting to prove that my English "was good enough" to be in mainstream classes instead of ESL, but my situation did not improve after exiting the program. I had teachers who were not culturally aware, which affected me in ways I could never have imagined.

I'll never forget a comment from a teacher whose class I enjoyed. As each student took a turn sharing which hospital they were born in during the labor and delivery lesson, I couldn't wait for my turn. As soon as I shared that I was born in Rwanda, my teacher said, "Oh, I can picture your mother giving birth in the bushes."

At first, I froze. I didn't know what to say, but moments later, as the classroom laughter settled, I responded, "I was actually born in a hospital, not in the bushes." It was painful because I liked her class, and that moment changed everything. In this case, my teacher made assumptions about me and did not pause to question where her comment came from. I am certain it was her "understanding" of Africa, but I clearly took offense to her comment and became closed off for the rest of the school year. These experiences are more common than we think, and our students suffer because a simple thoughtless comment can cause students to be less likely to engage, feel welcome, and feel safe.

Fast forward to a few years ago when I taught alongside colleagues from different backgrounds. It was essential for me to show up authentically and develop connections to learn about each other. I openly learned from and taught other educators so that more students do not have to experience cultural insensitivity and unawareness and deal with the lifelong effects. I worked with a teacher who considered herself an ally, but her words and actions proved otherwise. For example, she commented about how my hair was "messy" when it was in an Afro. She dedicated most of her time to working on social justice issues. I grew mistrustful toward her and questioned if her social justice efforts were just performative.

Cultural competency goes beyond what we say or do publicly. It is how we think, what we say behind closed doors when no "outsider" is around, and most importantly, how we navigate cultural engagements with people of different backgrounds. As important as it is to take cultural competence surveys, both teacher and student versions, we must do the internal work. Our thoughts continue to influence our actions, whether directly or indirectly, and we owe it to our students and the world to do the hard work. The reward is much greater than the discomfort that comes with unlearning problematic ideologies.

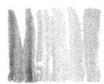

Being culturally competent entails having a clear set of values and beliefs, along with the attitudes, behaviors, policies, and structures that allow you to function effectively across cultural boundaries. You must 1) appreciate diversity, 2) self-evaluate, 3) handle the dynamics of difference, 4) learn about and institutionalize cultural norms, and 5) adjust to the varied cultural backgrounds of the people you serve. It takes time and practice to master. In order to benefit your students and create an inclusive environment, you must have the courage to confront your own fears, feelings of vulnerability, and prejudices. When providing equal opportunities for all students to learn, it is crucial to offer a platform to those whose views have been overlooked in the past. It takes planning and the right resources to construct and facilitate multicultural education environments. We, as educators, can prioritize our students and work to create a new, better world for us all. We must work on ourselves first and show our students our dedication to meeting their emotional, intellectual, and cultural needs in the classroom—and beyond.

PUT ANTI-RACIST PEDAGOGY INTO PRACTICE

T HE PRINCIPLES OF diversity, equality, inclusion, and accessibility (DEIA) are difficult for many teachers to put into practice. Additionally, in some areas, it is a "taboo" subject and even harder for teachers to seek equity training due to current political conflicts surrounding social justice-oriented curricula. Some teachers struggle to create a secure, welcoming environment for their students because of policy and practice discrepancies, and they anticipate resistance from various stakeholders, including leadership, parents, students, and their colleagues. Teachers must continue to promote efforts and implement anti-racist pedagogies to address equity gaps, develop an equality mindset, and create brave classrooms that address social justice concerns, regardless of the political limitations. We owe that to our students—to create a world that normalizes cultural and linguistic diversity.

Adopting an anti-racist pedagogy helps to negate the effects of racial ideologies on teacher rhetoric. Racialized students need instructors who will uphold their cultures while simultaneously valuing and affirming their linguistic diversity. More significantly, students want teachers who will challenge racial and linguistic injustices. Consider these calls to action:

- Integrate racialized students' colonial history.

- Design curricula that connect language and learning to larger political struggles.

- Recognize, acknowledge, and address language-based injustices inherent to colonialism, slavery, and other historical injustices that still play a role in today's issues.

- Create lessons and activities that take into account students' backgrounds and knowledge.

Our goal is to educate all students—including racialized students—in ways they deserve.

APPENDIX A

FROM HACK 1

APPENDIX A.1: SMART GOALS EXAMPLE

EXAMPLE: CREATE A SMART Goals activity based on the brave spaces rules you and your students developed (for your secondary school classroom).

Introduce the activity: Setting goals for ourselves is important if we want to improve as individuals. We all have the ability to become better people and to treat others the way we would want to be treated. Here is a list of the brave space elements (feel free to add your own): respect, vulnerability, kindness, active listening, patience, truthfulness, and speaking up. You can choose to set a goal around each one, depending on how much time you plan to spend on it during this school year and how you plan to measure your progress toward your goals.

Activity directions:

1. Ask students to reflect on their current behaviors, characteristics, or values and then set four or five goals in the areas they need to work on during the school year.

2. Ensure they make specific statements, and add a timeline and a way to measure their success.

3. They can choose to create a table, a digital vision board, or another shared document, as long as it can be updated with their progress over time.

4. Share an example that you created, and then allow them enough time to reflect on the activity before they share their work with you (such as in a shared document on the cloud). This will allow you to keep track of their progress, be an "accountability buddy," and leave feedback when necessary.

5. Remind students that they are responsible for reviewing their goals during the school year, making notes about their development, and tracking their achievement.

6. Share a rubric that shows how you will grade this project (emphasizing that students who update their documents over time and demonstrate progress with their goals will get full credit). You can also consider including this piece in the process of creating report cards.

EXAMPLE OF STUDENT GOAL SHEET

Reflection	SMART goal	Timeline	Student progress tracking (monthly check-ins)	Teacher feedback
Sometimes I listen to respond and do not fully understand what others are saying.	I plan to **actively listen** to my classmates when they speak.	Entire school year		
I have a hard time understanding ideas and experiences that are different from mine.	I will be more **open-minded** so I can better understand my classmates.	Entire school year		
I rarely ask questions because I often think people do not want to be asked about their backgrounds or experience.	I will be more intentional about asking questions and seeking guidance when I lack appropriate language to **ask questions** that may be sensitive.	Entire school year		
I often keep things to myself because I do not think others understand me.	I will slowly work on my **vulnerability** and connect more with others.	Entire school year		
I do not like apologizing when I offend others because it makes me uncomfortable.	I plan to **take accountability** for my actions, apologize when I am wrong, and be comfortable with discomfort.	Entire school year		

Image A.A.1.a: An example of a student goal sheet with space for tracking and teacher feedback.

WEEKLY JOURNAL PROMPT MODEL

Weekly Journal Prompt	Instructional Guide	Culturally Inclusive, Responsive, and Relevant Pedagogy
At the beginning of class, give students some questions to think about as they write in their journals. Ask them to:	Students will silently think and reflect on their lives and learn to express themselves through writing.	**Resources:** For writers who need extra support, provide translation resources if available.
Tell a short story about the things that matter to you the most and what makes you unique. *Write a letter to yourself for you to read in five years.*	Students will reflect on their responses and comment on their growth over time.	**Goals:** Students write a draft of their ideas in their home language, then translate them as much as possible for the journal activity.
After students finish their journals, they can share in small groups, and then, if comfortable, with the entire class. Gather all the journals at the end of the activity. Repeat the activity weekly and note (with the students) how their responses have changed throughout the school year.		Provide feedback in students' journals in multiple languages, if possible (if you are multilingual). Let students share with others in small, same-language groups.

Image A.A.1.b: A weekly journal prompt model.

APPENDIX A.2: EXCERPT FROM INCLUSIVE LESSON PLAN FOR MS. IRVIN'S SIXTH THROUGH EIGHTH GRADE

Lesson Plan Week 2 – Day 5

Morning Meeting (1–2 min.): **DREAAM Chant** (DREAAM is an organization that amplifies excellence in achievement, engagement, and overall wellness among youth.)

Affirmations (1 min.) 3-peat:

I am every great thing! I am able, I am smart. I am ready for whatever the day brings!

Sight Word Practice (15 min.):
Writing dictated sentences (20 min.). Started by teacher; finished by class.

Long "i" sounds with "igh"

10-minute stretch break

Ms. Clarisa /Mr. Kente's time
Read Aloud: comprehension, vocabulary, and fluency
Sulwe by Lupita Nyong'o (11 min.)
https://www.youtube.com/watch?v=vujbTOuzg2Q
Find the sight words in the read-aloud, and discuss (5–7 min.)
"Eyes closed" all sight work review and flash cards for Wednesday practice (5–7 min.)

15-minute recess & snack

Wind-down breathing exercise
https://www.youtube.com/watch?v=jKSkAtFUjo0
Note: As demonstrated in this excerpt from her lesson plan, Ms. Irvin makes time for students to collect themselves and promotes positive affirmations at the start of the lesson and

throughout—from chanting to affirming themselves and taking stretching and breathing breaks. This approach centers students and their overall well-being.

APPENDIX B

FROM HACK 3

APPENDIX B.1: RESEARCH PROJECT TO ADDRESS A SOCIAL PROBLEM

(An example activity for a high school classroom such as social studies or language arts.)

Objective: Students will learn how to conduct short- and long-term research projects to answer a question or address a social problem. They should understand when to limit or expand a topic, integrate knowledge from multiple sources, and demonstrate comprehension.

As part of a social change unit, twelfth graders conduct independent research on a particular policy. Encourage students to visit websites, read reputable blogs and articles, watch news and video clips, conduct social media conversation analysis, and listen to podcasts and other sources in English, as well as in their home languages. This lesson also serves native English speakers.

Note: Information must be available to students in all of their languages. Students can use the internet to find diverse multilingual resources that will help them make a case for their topic.

APPENDIX B.2: WORKING WITH A LANGUAGE PARTNER

Objective: Students summarize their findings after investigating a subject and effectively communicate ideas and information.

Activity directions:

1. Instruct students to conduct research on a country of their choice as part of a lesson that combines social studies, reading, or writing.

2. Give students a clear rubric, guidelines, and expectations—and go over the details with them to clear up confusion.

3. Allow students to conduct research on these nations using websites written in multiple languages.

4. Ask students to take notes in their home language as well as in English.

5. Ensure they have access to the necessary resources (such as the internet, a mobile device, a dictionary, or a vocabulary sheet). Students must be well-versed in significant and relevant information about that country. Utilizing student-friendly websites and taking notes in multiple languages aids all students in articulating their knowledge in writing.

6. Grade them according to the rubric you created and provide helpful feedback when necessary.

APPENDIX B.3: THE MIRROR
OR WINDOW ACTIVITY

Activity: Check out the article "Mirrors, Windows, and Sliding Glass Doors" by Rudine Sims Bishop.

Directions for the teacher:

- Make sure you have an account with a digital platform that allows you to poll students anonymously, such as Kahoot!

- Make a survey asking, "Do you see yourself in this writing, or does it reflect what you see elsewhere?" Include the options "window" and "mirror."

- Pick a book or article to discuss with your class.

- Read the material and highlight anything that could serve as a window or a mirror for your class. Providing a sample of the text can help ESL students break down the material into more manageable chunks and improve their understanding. Keep in mind that the "need to know" information in the text should be preemptively highlighted if there are any language learners in the class.

- Introduce the concept of windows and mirrors to the class. Ensure that all students have access to the text on their mobile devices.

- Ask students to do any required research on the author(s) of the piece and its historical context, or you can save time by providing them access to that knowledge.

- Students should contrast their identification groupings with the author's (e.g., race, ethnicity, gender, sexual orientation, immigration status, class, ability, religion).

What common identities exist? Which identities do not overlap? Think about intersectionality here.

- Students should read the entire text. They can read the paragraph again if they need extra time or additional support.

- Evaluate their comprehension of the reading by asking them for a quick summary of the main points.

- Activate the Kahoot! poll on the classroom screen as you walk around the room to ensure that all students have a summary written.

- Students should have their phone or other device ready to participate (load the poll access code and ask students to choose a pseudonym).

- Go over participation rules (time to be allocated to respond, not sharing the answer aloud).

- Click to display the first poll question (ensure that everyone can see it without issues).

- With each question, students should decide if the text extract serves as a window or a mirror for them.

- At the end of each question, the Kahoot! poll should share results, and after the final question—the top three students will be displayed as the activity champions.

- Debrief by discussing the poll results (you can also choose for students to debrief in small groups).

- During the discussion, remind students to support their responses with text-based evidence. Consider the question: Why did you choose this window?

- Wrap up by explaining why everyone's answers differed and tie it all together back to the text.

APPENDIX B.4: CRITICAL BOOK REVIEW ESSAY

(This can be used with upper-grade levels or adjusted accordingly for lower grades.)

Activity: Critical essay on a book (5–8 pages, single-spaced).

Objective: This helps students put their critical skills to the test and also uses their student voice and choice. Encourage language learners to use multilingual resources or their home languages to complete the project.

Directions for students:

- Review a scholarly book on the subject of exploring race in education. Choose a book from the class reading list or suggest one of your own. Audiobooks are okay. You will need four to six extra sources.

- Derive no more than two sources from class discussions or presentations.

- This project requires you to write a critical evaluation that analyzes how the researcher approaches race and education. You should not only paraphrase the author's arguments; instead, you should examine or criticize their methodology and take a stance.

- Be sure to start your essay with a clear question and utilize this question as your guide throughout.

- You are obligated to read the book.

- Your answer must contain analysis and criticism of the concepts presented.

- Depending on the length of your work, your summary may consist of no more than two or three short paragraphs. Devote the majority of your work to analysis and criticism of the book.

- I will grade your papers based on how well you show a knowledge of the ideas and arguments in the text, as well as how clearly and precisely you communicate the relationship between race and education.

APPENDIX C

FROM HACK 4

APPENDIX C.1: UNDERSTANDING INDIVIDUALS WITH DISABILITIES

Activity: This lesson teaches students about people with disabilities and how to interact with them in a caring manner.

Objective: Students will improve their understanding of people with disabilities and investigate appropriate communication practices for their peers and others with disabilities.

Pre-work/homework: All students research disabilities, collaborate on the classroom shared document, and organize information about autism, deafness, cerebral palsy, Down syndrome, intellectual disability, blindness, dyslexia, muscular dystrophy, and more. They can get help from their parents, ask questions in the community, or visit a local library. Do this a week before the assignment is officially distributed.

Pre-work directions:

- Look up the definition of "disability." Use the internet and ask questions. (You can also choose to collaborate with classmates.)
- What kind of physical disabilities are there?

- What are your worries regarding specific disabilities?
- What are the particular conditions associated with the different disabilities?
- What are the most effective methods of communicating with people who have disabilities?
- How can we educate others around us?

In-class group activity:

- Break students into groups and assign each one a topic for study, such as autism, deafness, cerebral palsy, Down syndrome, intellectual disability, blindness, dyslexia, or muscular dystrophy. Each group will assign one representative to take notes and another one to report back to the class.
- Before learning more about people with this disability, ask students to reflect on if they have preconceived notions about them.
- How has their understanding of this disability changed their perspective?
- Consider the following while presenting your topic to your group: What are the most important facts concerning this disability? What are the most prevalent everyday problems for someone with this disability? How can you assist someone with this disability? How can someone with this disability help you?
- After completing the task, please share your thoughts with the rest of the class.
- As a final product, students should submit their research in a creative digital report or a written paper for credit.
- **Thinking ahead:** How can we be more considerate of others in the future—in the classroom and beyond?

APPENDIX C.2: APP DEVELOPMENT CHALLENGE (STORYBOARDING) EXAMPLE

Create this project with a publicly available storyboarding app that you can download.

Week 1: Start

- Offer an option: the Community Challenge or the App Design Challenge.
- Learn the basics of coding (what is coding, what can it do, generic examples).
- Understand the objectives and rationale for this task.
- Provide a subject.
- Do pre-work (brainstorming community concerns, how can an app alleviate difficulties and solve issues).
- Decide if you will work alone, in groups, or in partnerships.
- Form teams and start an investigation into the chosen task (Journal of App Design).
- Determine how teams are going to work.

Week 2: Keynote prototype

- Display a few prototype examples.
- Review the app's (such as Keynote) prototype process.
- Go over the basics of the app.
- Ask students to imagine their application (features, pictures, shapes).
- Allocate time for them to brainstorm ideas for their app.
- Teach them how to connect with Keynote, explore app design, start storyboarding, and construct a prototype in Keynote.

See a teacher's example of a prototype build-out in Images A.C.2.a and A.C.2.b

BACKGROUND & ISSUE

Less commonly taught languages (African languages)
Lack of representation
Bridging the Black and African communities

SOLUTION

App: SWAHILING
Increase representation of Pan-African languages
Create safe and brave spaces
Provide resources
Bridge the gap
Create opportunities to learn and network

LEARN

Learn Swahili at the tip of your fingers!
Pace your learning
Set goals and accomplish them
Get help from native speakers

NETWORK

Add friends
Domestic connections
International connections
Attend networking events

EXPERIENCE

Build a community
Study abroad
Scholarship opportunities

Images A.C.2.a: The teacher's planning and prototype images of the SWAHILING app.

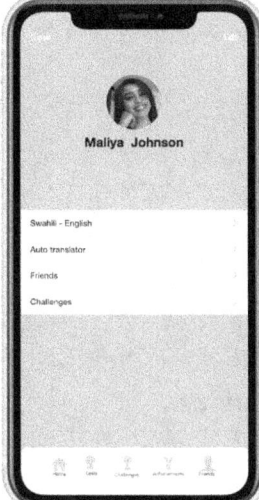 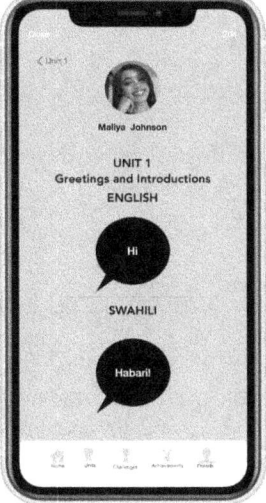 

Image A.C.2.b

Week 3: Review, consider, and research

- Connect the creation of apps and code to problem-solving.

- What other applications exist that are like yours?

- Where can you find support? Check out Swift playgrounds, the Everyone Can Code curriculum, and the App Design Journal.

- Practice using Keynote.

- Pitch using app clips.

Week 4: Problem-solving in action

- What issue is your app attempting to address?

- How is it resolved by the app?

- What are the most crucial characteristics of your app?

- If you had thirty seconds, what would you show your friends?

- Clips can teach you how to make an app pitch video.

Week 5: Celebrate the students' final developments

- Share proposal videos and prototypes with the larger community.

- Set aside time for comments and draft reviews.

- Gauge student interest after the project and see if they would like to develop functional applications.

APPENDIX D

FROM HACK 5

PEER REVIEW RUBRIC

Group being reviewed:
Topic/title:
Reviewer group members:
Date:

Question	Score	Comments
1. Is it clear what the topic is and its significance?		
2. Who exactly is the intended audience?		
3. Do you realize why these individuals undertook this project?		
4. What overall things did you learn from their outline?		
5. Are there sufficient examples/details?		
6. Do they compel you to want to know more about this topic?		
7. Do you understand what it would take to address this topic in a positive manner?		
8. Do you know who would be involved in addressing this topic (stakeholders)?		
9. Do you have a good sense of what those stakeholders would need to know or do?		
10. Do you feel moved to action at the end? Or do you have questions you want answered?		

Image A.D.1: Peer review rubric example.

APPENDIX E

FROM HACK 6

APPENDIX E.1: ACTIVITY EXAMPLE FOR EXAMINING STEREOTYPES IN LITERATURE

Activity: This activity helps students critically examine and respond to literature while emphasizing social justice.

Objectives: Students will consider, discuss, and write about stereotypes of gender, race, class, and other aspects of people's identities in literature. They will unpack the idea of "implicit" literary meanings and work collaboratively with their peers to get a deeper understanding of the books or articles they are reading. The issues covered in the reading should provoke critical thinking and inform personal responses from students.

Note: This activity engages students in social action projects as they read, understand, and acquire the necessary skills to address societal injustices. Students should apply what they have learned about critical reading to the critical analysis of other texts, particularly digital media.

1. Introduce the lesson to students by defining stereotypes and have students briefly research and share their understanding. This should

take about five to ten minutes, then follow up with a group activity with the following guiding questions:

a. What assumptions are in the texts we read?

b. How do these texts reinforce or challenge stereotypes?

c. How might critical reading make us better readers and better people overall?

d. How might readers combat prevalent literary stereotypes?

e. What parallels and distinctions can you see between reading books and reading other media?

f. Discuss the term "stereotype" as a class. Discuss what this term means to you and provide examples.

g. Divide the class into small groups to go further into stereotypes. They will choose an identity or group of people they want to research and present their findings on.

h. Each group should have a choice to use a digital platform to collaborate and compile their ideas into one medium. For instance, if they have iPads, they could use the Notes app or Pages to document their ideas.

i. Suggest incorporating visuals such as charts, tables, or Venn diagrams (see Image A.E.1). They must dedicate one side of the visuals to one group of people or individuals. For example, one side could be "fathers," and the other could be "mothers" or whatever other category they choose to explore.

j. Ask them to take five to ten minutes to fill out the information about each group—whatever they believe is stereotypically associated with either fathers or mothers. Scaffold the activity and then allow them to take ownership.

k. For the remaining time, ask them to write a few words that put fathers or mothers "outside the box" on the graphic or visual they are creating.

l. As a class, discuss what you believe makes fathers and mothers feel "inside" or "outside of the box." What is the connection between this and your previous conversation and knowledge of what a stereotype is? How do the students' experiences at home inform their understanding of these stereotypes? Do their home experiences highlight counter-narratives?

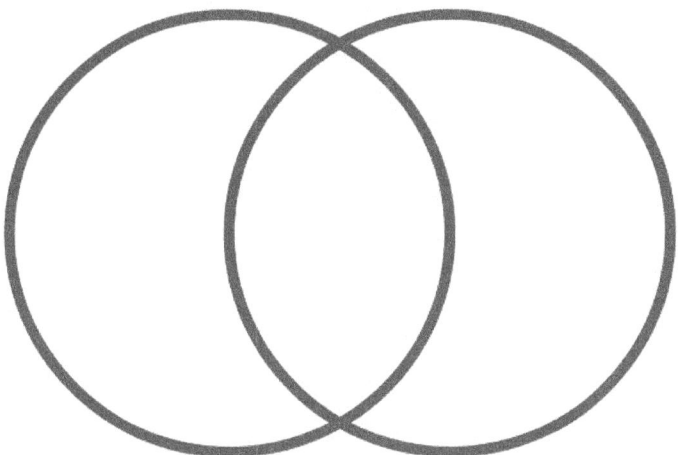

Image A.E.1: Venn diagram template

2. Build on this activity by making a list of themes (race, ethnicity, class, gender, or gender identity) so the class can study stereotypes at a different level and through an intersectionality lens.

    a. Create a table with the heading at the top for each category.

    b. Make another table for "other stereotypes."

    c. Discuss if a book, article, author, or character perpetuates or challenges a stereotype.

    d. Reflect on the visuals you've created as a class and discuss what this activity has taught you about literary stereotypes, how to decipher them, and how to craft critical counterarguments. Ask your students what they think about subliminal messages they saw.

APPENDIX E.2: ACTIVITY EXAMPLE TO EXAMINE STEREOTYPES IN MOVIES

Activity: How do movies portray millennials? This activity encourages students to think critically about the content they consume regularly and gain skills to define problematic messages that reproduce bias in our society.

Activity guidelines: Examine a relatively recent film. You will present your discussion of the movie to the class. Your presentation should last five to ten minutes. Schedule a presentation time and be ready to present to the class about how movies portray (or fail to portray) millennials in the United States (such as in society, social media, the workplace, and families).

Note: This project may consist of two parts (presentation and written responses).

The presentation must meet the following criteria:

1. Must present for five to ten minutes.

2. Share one or two quotes from the movie that you chose. Make sure you have proper access so you can

show the class relevant short clips (publicly available previews are okay).

3. Do not play offensive videos. You should watch the video in advance, know which scene to share, and only display the material that is pertinent to your presentation.

4. Cover the following subjects in your presentation:

    a. A synopsis of the film (under two minutes).

    b. The appearance of stereotyped characters (generational prejudice, gender stereotypes, cultural expectations).

    c. How are members of previous generations depicted?

    d. Do you think it is a proper portrayal of millennials? Why or why not?

    e. Other opinions or remarks on the movie as a whole?

FROM HACK 7

APPENDIX F.1: A SERIES OF LESSONS BASED ON IDENTITY, DIVERSITY, JUSTICE, AND ACTION (IDJA) STANDARDS

Identity

1. Students will develop positive social identities based on their membership in multiple groups in society.

2. Students will develop language skills and historical and cultural knowledge that affirms and accurately describes their membership in multiple identity groups.

3. Students will recognize that people's multiple identities interact and create unique and complex individuals.

4. Students will express pride, confidence, and healthy self-esteem without denying the value and dignity of other people.

5. Students will recognize traits of the dominant culture, their home culture, and other cultures

and understand how they negotiate their identity in multiple spaces.

6. Consider activities to help students grapple with the idea of "identity," discovering themselves, and understanding each other.

Diversity

1. Students will express comfort with people who are both similar to and different from them and engage respectfully with all people.

2. Students will develop language and knowledge to accurately and respectfully describe how people (including themselves) are both similar to and different from each other and others in their identity groups.

3. Students will respectfully express curiosity about the history and lived experiences of others and will exchange ideas and beliefs in an open-minded way.

4. Students will respond to diversity by building empathy, respect, understanding, and connection.

5. Students will examine diversity in social, cultural, political, and historical contexts rather than in ways that are superficial or oversimplified.

Justice

1. Students will recognize stereotypes and relate to people as individuals rather than as representatives of groups.

2. Students will recognize unfairness on the individual level (e.g., biased speech) and injustice at the institutional or systemic level (e.g., discrimination).

3. Students will analyze the harmful impact of bias and injustice on the world, historically and today.

4. Students will recognize that power and privilege influence relationships on interpersonal, intergroup, and institutional levels. They will consider how they have been affected by those dynamics.

5. Students will identify figures, groups, events, and various strategies and philosophies relevant to the history of social justice around the world.

Action

1. Students will express empathy when viewing the exclusion or mistreatment of people because of their identities and concern when they themselves experience bias.

2. Students will recognize their responsibility to stand up to exclusion, prejudice, and injustice.

3. Students will speak up with courage and respect when they or someone else has been hurt or wronged by bias.

4. Students will make principled decisions about when and how to take a stand against bias and injustice in their everyday lives and will do so despite negative peer or group pressure.

5. Students will plan and carry out collective action against bias and injustice in the world and will evaluate which strategies are most effective.

APPENDIX F.2: A SOCIAL JUSTICE PROJECT ASSESSMENT

In order to get a good grade on their social justice projects, students had to show:

1. Personal growth (see the following reflection for details)

2. Professional growth (with regard to expanding the social justice conversation)

3. Sophistication/rigor of the final product

The course's goal was for students to grow personally and professionally, and the course's products and presentation were its means of achieving that goal.

Reflection on the project planning process

Students posted two to three sentences reflecting on each of the following categories:

- **Audience (layered audiences):** Why and how did you select their demographic?

- **Consider what is not being discussed:** Why did someone leave it out (specificity, intersectionality, delving deeper, considering geography)?

- **Personal connection to the subject (positionality):** Are you learning anything new or understanding other people's perspectives?

- **Product category:** What makes a documentary, website, or lesson plan the most effective for achieving your goals?

- **Language:** How did you select a form of communication with your audience? Was the language formal or informal? Did you consider different languages or dialects?

- **Effectiveness of message:** How does it transform what many people in society have already done or said?

- **Call to action:** Does your call to action correspond with course concepts? If so, which ones are which?

- **Challenges:** What obstacles did you face in creating this project, such as choosing between an ally and an accomplice and making important decisions?

- **Choose one challenge and share how you overcame it:** Describe a choice you made and the reasoning behind it.

Tip: Guide students to use a shared document to take notes on each category so they can be concise and specific when summarizing their findings.

APPENDIX G

FROM HACK 8

APPENDIX G.1: ALTERNATIVE EVALUATION FORM FOR CULTURAL COMPETENCE

See an example of an alternative evaluation form in Image A.G.1. Use the questions as a guide and template to evaluate your cultural fluency. You can also develop student versions of this evaluation form.

Question	Rate 1–5
How self-aware are you when it comes to how you treat students who belong to racial or ethnic minorities? (Use a scale from 1 to 5 to rate yourself.)	
Have you ever confronted a racist mindset, either in another person or in yourself?	
How aware are you of your own potential ethnocentrism while interacting with students of other cultural backgrounds?	
Do you have the ability to communicate and engage with students and their families from diverse cultures in their native tongue?	
If you have immigrant students, do you have any idea of their origin or the conditions under which they may have migrated?	
Do you take into account the religious practices of your students even if they vary from your own?	
Have you ever taken classes or otherwise educated yourself on cross-cultural issues? How well do you feel you can use that knowledge in a conversation?	
How would you rate your ability to engage with others outside of your cultural group?	
To what extent do you place a premium on the meta skills of compassion, neutrality, nonjudgment, acceptance, and listening?	
How would you rate your ability to engage with others outside of your cultural group?	
Have you spoken to your leadership or colleagues about any problems with cross-cultural communication that may have come up in the classroom?	
How does your background in culture influence your judgment when you're dealing with culturally and linguistically diverse students and colleagues?	
Do you often participate in events or activities with colleagues and students from racialized groups? If not, why?	

Image A.G.1: An alternative cultural competence evaluation form.

APPENDIX G.2: PHASES OF THE CULTURAL COMPETENCE CONTINUUM

1. **Awareness:** This phase involves gaining knowledge about the cultures and values of different groups of people. Individuals become familiar with different cultural norms and values and learn to recognize and appreciate the diversity of different cultures.

2. **Understanding:** This phase builds on the knowledge gained in the awareness phase and involves gaining a deeper understanding of different cultures. Individuals learn more about the history, experiences, and perspectives of different groups of people.

3. **Application:** This phase involves applying the knowledge and understanding of different cultures to real-life situations. Individuals learn how to respect and interact with people from different backgrounds and effectively communicate with them.

4. **Integration:** The final phase involves integrating the knowledge, understanding, and application of different cultures into one's own life and work. Individuals strive to create a sense of inclusion, collaboration, and mutual respect among different groups of people.

APPENDIX G.3: BUILD A VISUAL MENTAL MAP

A visual mental map allows you to look at your beliefs and values in a materialized way. People who keep vision boards or other forms of materialization of their goals and values are more likely to remember their focus and keep working toward their desired achievements.

Image A.G.3 shows an example of the visual mental map I created when I was taking a course on evaluation, which required me to reflect on my beliefs and values in order to promote equitable evaluation. You may want to keep a copy of yours in your room near your desk as a daily reminder.

These are the questions that informed my statements:

- Why do you consider yourself a social justice and student-focused educator?
- What prompted you to choose this path?
- What values drive you?
- Who or what has an impact on your practice (books, researchers, practitioners, colleagues), and why?
- What experiences have shaped your current beliefs?

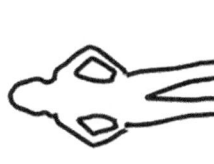

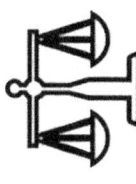

I value language and culture. I believe it is a huge part of one's identity.

I want to be a part of the change that will promote equity for everyone.

I have developed my beliefs about the world by unlearning false information and becoming a seeker of knowledge/researcher.

I want to contribute to the betterment of CLDs' academic experiences and collaborate with other educators to provide resources and support to them, their parents and communities.

I am influenced by my own experiences and injustices/malpractices I have witnessed.

I value quality education, access to resources and opportunities for racialized communities.

I value human experiences (qualitative research).

Fields I draw from: linguistics, second language learning, sociolinguistics, multilingualism, language and literacy, and education technology.

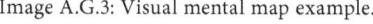

Image A.G.3: Visual mental map example.

REFERENCES

Introduction

"Educational Researcher." http://Edr.sagepub.com/Content/41/3/93. Accessed Feb. 14, 2023. https://web.stanford.edu/class/linguist159/restricted/readings/Paris2012.pdf.

Flores, Nelson, and Jonathan Rosa. 2015. "Undoing Appropriateness: Raciolinguistic Ideologies and Language Diversity in Education." *Harvard Educational Review* 85, no. 2: 149–171.

Gay, Geneva. 2021. "Culturally Responsive Teaching." *Handbook of Urban Education*: 212–233.

National Center for Education Statistics (NCES), a part of the U.S. Department of Education. Accessed Feb. 14, 2023. https://nces.ed.gov/.

HACK 1

Crenshaw, Kimberlé. 2018. "Demarginalizing the Intersection of Race and Sex: A Black Feminist Critique of Antidiscrimination Doctrine, Feminist Theory, and Antiracist Politics [1989]." *Feminist Legal Theory*: 57–80.

"Flashpoints." 2017. *Safe Spaces, Brave Spaces*.

HACK 2

Bovill, C. 2013. "Students and staff co-creating curricula: a new trend or an old idea we never got around to implementing?" https://eprints.gla.ac.uk/82348/1/82348.pdf.

"National Center on Safe Supportive Learning Environments (NCSSLE)." n.d. Safesupportivelearning.ed.gov.

"What Makes Great Teachers Great?" 2004. *The Chronicle of Higher Education.* April 9, 2004. http://www.chronicle.com/article/what-makes-great-teachers-great.

HACK 3

Bourdieu, P. 1977. "The Economics of Linguistic Exchanges." *Social Science Information* 16, no. 6 (January): 645–68. https://doi.org/10.1177/053901847701600601.

Conteh, Jean. 2015. "'Funds of Knowledge' for Achievement and Success: Multilingual Pedagogies for Mainstream Primary Classrooms in England." *International Perspectives on ELT Classroom Interaction*, 49–63. https://doi.org/10.1057/9781137340733_4.

Freeman, David, and Yvonne Freeman. 1999. "Effective Practices for English Language Learners." *Educational Considerations* 26, no. 2 (April). https://doi.org/10.4148/0146-9282.1349.

García, Ofelia, Susana Ibarra Johnson, Kate Seltzer, and Guadalupe Valdés. 2017. *The Translanguaging Classroom: Leveraging Student Bilingualism for Learning.* Caslon.

García, Ofelia, and Angel M. Y. Lin. 2017. "Translanguaging in Bilingual Education." *Bilingual and Multilingual Education*, 117–30. https://doi.org/10.1007/978-3-319-02258-1_9.

Learning for Justice. 1991. "Learning for Justice – Education Resources." https://www.learningforjustice.org/.

NCTE. 2019. https://ncte.org/.

Paris, Django. 2012. "Culturally Sustaining Pedagogy: A Needed Change in Stance, Terminology, and Practice." *Educational Researcher* 41, no. 3. https://doi.org/10.3102/0013189X12441244.

Seltzer, Kate. 2019. "Reconceptualizing 'Home' and 'School' Language: Taking a Critical Translingual Approach in the English Classroom." *TESOL Quarterly* 53, no. 4 (August): 986–1007. https://doi.org/10.1002/tesq.530.

HACK 4

"EdTech Classroom." n.d. Accessed Feb. 14, 2023. https://edtech-class.com/.

Office of Educational Technology. 2016. "Guiding Principles for Use of Technology with Early Learners." https://tech.ed.gov/earlylearning/principles/.

Reading Rockets. 2018. "The State of Learning Disabilities: Understanding the 1 in 5." June 2, 2018. https://www.readingrockets.org/articles/researchbytopic/33823.

U.S. Department of Education. 2017. "Individuals with Disabilities Education Act." Ed.gov. https://sites.ed.gov/idea/.

HACK 5

"Designing, Launching, and Implementing High Quality Learning Opportunities for Students that Advance Scientific Thinking." Accessed Feb. 15, 2023. https://onlinelibrary.wiley.com/doi/abs/10.1002/tea.21329.

Greer, G. B., et al. 2009. *Culturally Responsive Mathematics Education*. Routledge.

National Education Association. 2022. https://www.nea.org/.

HACK 6

Villegas, Ana María, and Tamara Lucas. 2002. "Preparing Culturally Responsive Teachers." *Journal of Teacher Education* 53, no. 1 (January): 20–32. https://doi.org/10.1177/0022487102053001003.

HACK 7

Chartock, Roselle. 2010. *Strategies and Lessons for Culturally Responsive Teaching: A Primer for K–12*. Pearson.

Ryan, Richard M, and Edward L. Deci. 2017. *Self-Determination Theory: Basic Psychological Needs in Motivation, Development, and Wellness*. Guilford Press.

HACK 8

Gallegos, Joseph S., Cherie Tindall, and Sheila A. Gallegos. 2018. "The Need for Advancement in the Conceptualization of Cultural Competence." *Advances in social work* 9: 51–62.

Hamdan, Suha, and Roland Sintos Coloma. 2022. "Assessing Teachers' Cultural Competency." *Educational Foundations* 35, no. 1: 108–28. https://eric.ed.gov/?id=EJ1358841.

SNEAK PEEK

"**A**T RISK."
      "Low."
      "Lazy."
"Unmotivated."
"Not smart."
"Apartment kids."
"Title I kids."
"We already know where he will end up after high school."
"Her parents don't care about her."
"Education is not part of their culture."
"If they don't address it at home, there's nothing we can do."
"They don't want to succeed."
"He's just mimicking the problem behaviors he sees at home."
"This school is not a good fit for him."

If you have ever worked in a school, you have probably heard some of these coded labels and phrases; perhaps you've even spoken them. While well-intentioned and unassuming educators often state such assumptions and judgments, these phrases sum up deficit thinking.

"Deficit thinking" has become a wildly popular term in education. But what does it mean, and what does it look like in schools? We asked educators to define it for us, and we ultimately came to the following shared definition:

A distorted lens focused on student weaknesses that blames students and their families for student difficulties rather than acknowledging the impact of our practices and broader structural inequities.

Let's break that down.

1. A distorted lens. Biases about student abilities color our world-view and warp our reality. They may stem from our upbringing, stereotypes we've encountered over time, or harmful generalizations that we believe. This is the unfortunate power of deficit thinking. The longer we operate from this distorted lens, the more data we find that confirms our false beliefs. And the longer we operate from this lens, the more students we fail.

2. Focused on student weaknesses. This emphasis on student weakness is especially present when working with minority groups and students from marginalized backgrounds. It's based on racism, classism, sexism, ableism, and eugenics. It targets those historically identified as "inferior" and "unwelcome" in schools.

3. That blames students and their families for student difficulties. Our educational system originally supported the idea that only White, middle-class, able-bodied males deserved an education. Cultural norms seemed to consider other qualities as a "weakness." (You'll learn more about that later.) By not valuing the strengths of all individuals, the blame began.

> "If my instruction benefits some students and not others, it has to be the student's fault, right?"
>
> "If some students know how to behave in my class, but others don't, it has to be the parents' fault, right?"

4. Rather than acknowledging the impact of our practices and broader structural inequities. School buildings and our larger society constantly contribute to and reinforce systemic racism and other-isms that impact our interactions with students. Blaming the students takes the responsibility off us.

Because this lens places all fault on the students, we lower our expectations for them, either intentionally or subconsciously. If we have low expectations for students, we aren't motivated to provide them with enrichment. We successfully allow ourselves to believe that we can do nothing to contribute to better outcomes. Students will always rise to the level of expectation we have set for them. If the expectation is low, they will only grow so much because they believe in our judgments.

Now that we understand how pervasive and harmful deficit thinking can be, you may ask what you can do to discard such a powerful ideology. Fortunately, many practices aid in dismantling deficit thinking. However, if we want to discard the deficit model, we must go through discomfort. We can no longer easily place blame on others. We must look at our practices critically and accept that we are the problem nine times out of ten—whether it is our inability to truly see our students or our habit of not taking the time to listen.

INTENDED AUDIENCE

This book is intended primarily for teachers, administrators, and school-based support staff such as school psychologists, counselors, and related service providers. It will also be helpful in teacher training programs or other graduate preparation courses that set the foundation for future educators. We designed this book for you if you work with students or plan to. It is chock-full of helpful information and tools to hack deficit thinking.

HOW TO USE THIS BOOK

This book will help you understand where deficit thinking stems from and why it is such a powerful narrative. Once we understand *why* we think the way we do, we can understand how to change our behaviors and unlearn harmful patterns. Dismantling deficit thinking depends on our ability to self-reflect and self-correct. We can change our thinking and behaviors to recognize and acknowledge strengths within ourselves, our students, and our schools—to better serve everyone.

We rely on a set of interviews we conducted with educators and input we received from Google Forms and questions posed on Twitter. While we also rely on best practices and frameworks identified by education researchers, we also build upon the words that came directly from people like you.

Hacking Deficit Thinking is 50 percent self-reflection and 50 percent actionable classroom and schoolwide practices. It allows us to identify and address deficit thinking within ourselves and our practices, and we need both to better serve our students.

BUY *HACKING DEFICIT THINKING*

AVAILABLE AT:
Amazon.com
10Publications.com
and bookstores near you

ABOUT THE AUTHOR

Kendra Nalubega-Booker is a mother, wife, educator, and lifelong learner. In her role as an Education Leadership Executive, she collaborates with K–12 and Higher Education leaders to bridge equity and access gaps and create inclusive learning experiences for all students. She is also a PhD candidate at the University of Illinois at Urbana-Champaign's Department of Curriculum and Instruction. She is a published author, and her research focuses on evaluating policies and practices, specifically the assessment of Black students' literacies in the US educational system, with an emphasis on language and culture.

Email: zamnalubega@gmail.com

ACKNOWLEDGMENTS

FIRST, I WANT to thank God for this opportunity to amplify my voice and give me the means to materialize my experience and expertise, as well as make my dreams come true. I have always had a passion for education since I could speak. I would play "teacher" instead of "house" with my friends and family growing up. I found so much joy in doing that, and parents in the community started sending their kids over to my mother's house so they could go to "school." I still crack myself up thinking about it, but looking back, I understand now that my purpose is in education. I have spent the last several years growing into it and finding different ways to contribute to the betterment of schooling systems, especially the student experience. Although I knew my passion and purpose at an early age, I did not always have resources or access, and God made a way.

This book is a huge accomplishment for me because I've always wanted to contribute to meaningful literature that inspires people to take action. During my time as a student, my experiences as a Black immigrant sparked my interest in social change that affected students like me and others who suffer at the hands of an inequitable schooling system. As an educator today, it unsettles me to know that racialized students still experience the same issues inside and outside the classroom, especially when it comes to their diverse cultures and linguistic practices. I am grateful to the scholars who have pushed for a shift in educational research and practice, including Dr. Arlette Ingram Willis, Dr. Patriann Smith, Dr. April Baker-Bell, Dr. Nelson Flores, Dr. Jonathan Rosa, Dr.

Adrienne Dixson, Dr. Gloria Ladson-Billings, Dr. Django Paris, Dr. Geneva Gay, Dr. Kimberlé Crenshaw, and many more!

I am grateful to Storm Booker, the world's most devoted husband, for always being there for me. We moved across the country with our toddler, got COVID, and started new roles while I was writing this book. You still motivated me, listened to my ideas, and offered constructive criticism. You are my biggest cheerleader, and you never let doubt get in my way because you are always there to remind me that I am capable, brilliant, and that my voice is needed. You pushed me to get some rest and take care of myself. You filled my cup when I was empty, and that allowed me to pour my all into this book. I love you beyond this lifetime and appreciate you deeply.

My firstborn, Stoney Booker, you are my motivation! Every time I felt like giving up, your smile, random hugs, and kisses kept me going. I hope to build a place where you can be yourself and flourish in ways you never thought possible. I want to raise a person who is proud of who they are, isn't afraid to take risks, and stands up for what's right.

A special thank you to my grandmother (may she rest peacefully), Nabawanuka Lutale, for nurturing my love for education, advocating for me, and teaching me to always do right by myself and everyone around me, because we all deserve to be seen, heard, and valued. For showing me what leadership looks like and for always being brave enough to say and do what others are afraid to.

I also want to thank my mother, Harriet Kayombya, for being my biggest fan, supporting my dreams, and never giving up on building a good life for my sister, brother, and me. Thank you for taking the risks that led me here. You are my reason, and I pray that I continue to make you proud. You have shown me that I can accomplish anything when I put my mind to it. For my sister, Sasha Namuwonge Mutesi, we share many overlapping experiences that continue to inspire my work. You were the first person who made me realize the importance of advocacy, which now extends to my little brother, Nelson Odwongo. You both inspire me to be the best big sister, and I hope to show you that you, too, can achieve your dreams.

With deep gratitude to Ms. Kellye Galvan and my sisters Alissa Irvin, Miche'le Johnson, and Char'Li Ali, three of the educators who have taken the time to mentor me and share their wisdom. I appreciate so much the opportunity to speak with you about how you incorporate diversity into the classroom. You all are some of the most intentional educators I know, and I admire the classroom experience you create for your students. You gave me a glimpse of what other classrooms could look like, and for that, I am grateful.

Thank you for always being there to pray for me, give me sound advice, and lend an ear when I needed one, Dr. Kenya Ayers-Palmore, my mentor-momma. You continue to have a huge impact on who I am becoming.

Thank you so much to Sherida Brett-Green for introducing me to Stefani Roth, who then brought me to Times 10 after several Zoom meetings filled with thought-provoking conversations. This opportunity would not have come to me at a better time if it hadn't been for you two. I am grateful to Mark Barnes for welcoming me with open arms and amplifying my voice through this platform. Thank you, Jen Z. Marshall, for being so supportive and assisting me in articulating my thoughts in an accessible, authentic manner. As this was my first book, I felt stuck at times about how to position content and determine what was enough or insufficient, and she made time to assist me throughout the process.

MORE FROM TIMES 10 PUBLICATIONS

Browse all titles at 10Publications.com

Hacking School Discipline

9 Ways to Create a Culture of Empathy & Responsibility Using Restorative Justice

By Nathan Maynard and Brad Weinstein

Reviewers proclaim this *Washington Post* Bestseller to be "maybe the most important book a teacher can read, a must for all educators, fabulous, a game changer!" Teachers and presenters Nathan Maynard and Brad Weinstein demonstrate how to eliminate punishment and build a culture of responsible students and independent learners in a book that will become your new blueprint for school discipline. Twenty-one straight months at #1 on Amazon, *Hacking School Discipline* is disrupting education like nothing we've seen in decades—maybe centuries.

Hacking Project Based Learning

10 Easy Steps to PBL and Inquiry in the Classroom

By Ross Cooper and Erin Murphy

As questions and mysteries around PBL and inquiry continue to swirl, experienced classroom teachers and school administrators Ross Cooper and Erin Murphy empower those intimidated by PBL to cry, "I can do this!" while providing added value for those who are already familiar with the process. *Hacking Project Based Learning* demystifies what PBL is all about with ten Hacks that construct a simple path that educators and students can easily follow to achieve success.

Browse all titles at 10Publications.com

Sanée Bell

Be Excellent on Purpose

Intentional Strategies for Impactful Leadership

By Sanée Bell

Excellence is a journey where one discovers who they are, what they value, and the principles that drive them. But it's not always easy for educators to rise above the fray and live a purposeful life. To *Be Excellent on Purpose* means making a plan for life and working the plan to make it a reality. In this inaugural book in the Lead Forward Series, teacher, author, presenter, and school leader Sanée Bell shares personal and professional stories and strategies that will make your leadership intentional and impactful.

Hacking Classroom Management

10 Ideas To Help You Become the Type of Teacher They Make Movies About

By Mike Roberts

Learn the ten ideas you can use today to create the classroom any great movie teacher would love. Utah English Teacher of the Year and sought-after speaker Mike Roberts brings you quick and easy classroom management Hacks that will make your classroom the place to be for all your students. He shows you how to create an amazing learning environment that makes discipline, rules, and consequences obsolete, no matter if you're a new teacher or a thirty-year veteran teacher.

Browse all titles at 10Publications.com

Hacking Teacher Burnout

8 Steps to Go From Isolated to Empowered so You Can Overcome Any Challenge

By Amber Harper

Teachers experience challenges such as distance learning, new technologies, higher expectations, discipline issues, and personal crises. Sound familiar? Veteran classroom teacher, podcaster, and Google trainer Amber Harper shares eight steps that shine a light on burnout and help teachers become BURNED-IN: fulfilled, happy, efficient, and effective in the classroom and in life. Take action based on your burnout type, thrive personally and professionally, and learn how to cope with any challenge.

Hacking Questions

11 Answers that Create a Culture of Inquiry in Your Classroom

By Connie Hamilton

Questions are the driving force of learning in classrooms, but teachers have questions about how to engage their students with the art of questioning. *Hacking Questions* digs into framing, delivering, and maximizing questions in the classroom to keep students engaged in learning. Known in education circles as the "Questioning Guru," Connie Hamilton shows teachers of all subjects and grades how to ask the questions that deliver not just answers but reflection, metacognition, and real learning.

Browse all titles at 10Publications.com

RESOURCES FROM TIMES 10 PUBLICATIONS

10Publications.com

Nurture your inner educator:
10publications.com/educatortype

Podcasts:

hacklearningpodcast.com
jamesalansturtevant.com/podcast

On Twitter:

@10Publications
@HackMyLearning
#Times10News
#RealPBL
@LeadForward2
#LeadForward
#HackLearning
#HackingLeadership
#MakeWriting
#HackingQs
#HackingSchoolDiscipline
#LeadWithGrace
#HackingSchoolLibraries

All things Times 10:

10Publications.com

TIMES 10 PUBLICATIONS provides practical solutions that busy educators can read today and use tomorrow. We bring you content from experienced teachers and leaders, and we share it through books, podcasts, webinars, articles, events, and ongoing conversations on social media. Our books and materials help turn practice into action. Stay in touch with us at 10Publications.com and follow our updates on Twitter @10Publications and #Times10News.